W9-CAJ-707

SLAVERY IN AMERICAN HISTORY

THE POLITICS
OF SLAVERY

FIERY NATIONAL DEBATES

FUELED BY THE SLAVE ECONOMY

LINDA JACOBS ALTMAN

FOREWORD BY SERIES ADVISOR
DR. HENRY LOUIS GATES, JR.

Enslow Publishers, Inc.

40 Industrial Road	PO Box 38
Box 398	Aldershot
Berkeley Heights, NJ 07922	Hants GU12 6BP
USA	UK

http://www.enslow.com

Library of Congress Cataloging-in-Publication Data

Altman, Linda Jacobs, 1943–
   The politics of slavery : fiery national debates fueled by the slave economy / by
Linda Jacobs Altman.
      v. cm. — (Slavery in American history)
   Includes bibliographical references and index.
   Contents: The beginnings of American slavery—From servants to
slaves—Slavery and the founding freedoms—Compromise and the Constitution—
Slavery in a growing nation—Missouri and the westward expansion—Slavery and
manifest destiny—North and South : a clash of cultures—The road to disunion.
   ISBN 0-7660-2150-5
   1. Slavery—Political aspects—United States—History—Juvenile literature.
2. Slavery—United States—History—Juvenile literature. 3. United States—Politics
and government—Juvenile literature. 4. United States—Race relations—Juvenile
literature. [1. Slavery. 2. United States—Politics and government. 3. Race relations.]
I. Title. II. Series.
E441.A5765 2004
326'.0973—dc22

                                                    2003026532

Printed in the United States of America

10 9 8 7 6 5 4 3 2 1

To Our Readers: We have done our best to make sure all Internet addresses in this book
were active and appropriate when we went to press. However, the author and the
publisher have no control over and assume no liability for the material available on those
Internet sites or on other Web sites they may link to. Any comments or suggestions can
be sent by e-mail to comments@enslow.com or to the address on the back cover.

Illustration Credits: The Art Archive, p. 14; © Corbis, pp. 25, 93, 109; Enslow Publishers,
Inc., pp. 53, 69, 101; © Jane Reed, Harvard News Office, p. 5; National Archives and
Records Administration, p. 83; Courtesy New York Historical Society, reproduced from the
Dictionary of American Portraits, published by Dover Publications, Inc., in 1967, p. 106;
North Wind Picture Archives, pp. 11, 31, 46, 59, 73, 97, 103; Painting by Gilbert Stuart,
reproduced from the *Dictionary of American Portraits*, published by Dover Publications,
Inc., in 1967, p. 42; Painting by G.P.A. Healy, reproduced from the *Dictionary of American
Portraits*, published by Dover Publications, Inc., in 1967, p. 79; Reproduced from the
Collections of the Library of Congress, pp. 1, 3, 6–7, 22, 38, 110; Snark/Art Resource, NY,
p. 75.

Cover Illustration: Reproduced from the Collections of the Library of Congress.

✦ C O N T E N T S ✦

American Slavery's Undying Legacy

While the Thirteenth Amendment outlawed slavery in the United States in 1865, the impact of that institution continued to be felt long afterward, and in many ways is still being felt today. The broad variety of experiences encompassed within that epoch of American history can be difficult to encapsulate. Enslaved, free, owner, trader, abolitionist: each "category" hides a complexity of experience as varied as the number of individuals who occupied these identities.

One thing is certain: in spite of how slavery has sometimes been portrayed, very few, if any, enslaved blacks were utter victims who quietly and passively accepted such circumstances. Those who claimed ownership over Africans and African Americans used violence, intimidation, and other means to wield a great degree of power and control. But as human beings—and as laborers within an economic system that depended on labor—all enslaved blacks retained varying degrees of agency within that system.

The "Slavery in American History" series provides a strong and needed overview of the most important aspects of American slavery, from the first transport of African slaves to the American colonies, to the long fight for abolition, to the lasting impact of slavery on America's economy, politics, and culture. Only by understanding American slavery and its complex legacies can we begin to understand the challenge facing not just African Americans, but all Americans: To make certain that our country is a living and breathing embodiment of the principles enunciated in the Constitution of the United States. Only by understanding the past can we mend the present and ensure the rights of our future generations.

—**Henry Louis Gates, Jr.**, *Ph.D., W.E.B. Du Bois Professor of the Humanities, Chair of the Department African and African-American Studies, Director of the W.E.B. Du Bois Institute for African and African-American Research, Harvard University.*

Dr. Henry Louis Gates, Jr., Series Advisor

Dr. Henry Louis Gates, Jr., is author of a number of books including: *The Trials of Phillis Wheatley: America's First Poet and Her Encounters with the Founding Fathers*, *The African-American Century* (with Cornel West), *Little Known Black History Facts*, *Africana: The Encyclopedia of the African American Experience*, *Wonders of the African*

World, *The Future of The Race* (with Cornel West), *Colored People: A Memoir*, *Loose Cannons: Notes on the Culture Wars*, *The Signifying Monkey: Towards A Theory of Afro-American Literary Criticism*, *Figures in Black: Words, Signs, and the Racial Self*, and *Thirteen Ways of Looking at a Black Man*.

Professor Gates earned his M.A. and Ph.D. in English Literature from Clare College at the University of Cambridge. Before beginning his work at Harvard in 1991, he taught at Yale, Cornell, and Duke universities. He has been named one of *Time* magazine's "25 Most Influential Americans," received a National Humanities Medal, and was elected to the American Academy of Arts and Letters.

THE BEGINNINGS OF AMERICAN SLAVERY

IN 1619, A DUTCH SHIP ARRIVED AT THE JAMESTOWN Colony in present-day Virginia. It carried human cargo, which the colonists gladly bought. In the process, the settlers began a tumultous era in American history.

The chief evidence of this sale was an entry in the journal of colonist John Rolfe: "About the last of August came a Dutch man of war [warship] that sold us twenty negroes."[1] This one sentence is the first known mention of the slave trade in what would become the United States.

Though slavery grew into an institution, some Americans were never quite comfortable with turning human beings into property. Conflicts over slavery played a central role in the political and economic development of the nation.

arrived in the New World in 1492. By the early 1500s, a steady stream of European settlers followed, drawn by the prospect of free land and a fresh start. In the Caribbean and South America, they found fertile soil and a tropical climate, ideal conditions for growing sugar cane and other warm-weather field crops. To make this large-scale agriculture profitable, planters needed a ready supply of cheap labor.

The Gold Coast slave traders gladly filled the need. In the process, they created the dreaded Middle Passage of what was often called the Triangle Trade: from Europe to Africa, then across the Atlantic to the Americas, and back again to Europe. The Middle Passage was the leg of the journey from Africa to the Americas where the slaves suffered in the hold of the ship for days on end.

Africans and the Slave Trade

Slavery existed in Africa long before the Europeans came, but it was not a business. Africans did not engage in the buying and selling of slaves for profit, nor did their economy depend upon slave labor. Perhaps most important of all, Africans did not single out a particular racial or ethnic group for enslavement.

They enslaved war captives, criminals, debtors, and social misfits. Sometimes, families gave children away to settle a debt or as part of a bridal dowry. These

Africans sometimes captured their own people and sold them to Europeans. However, many of the African slave traders did not realize that slavery in the New World was far more restrictive than the type of slavery that was practiced in Africa.

people were not free, but neither were they property in the sense that slaves would become property in the American colonies.

Slaves often lived with their masters as equals, or at least as respected and well-treated servants. Among the Ashanti of West Africa, slaves could marry, own property, and generally exercise a great deal of control over their own lives.

Without racism or a profit motive, slavery was only a minor part of traditional African life. Then the European traders came, their cargo holds filled with all manner of useful or beautiful things to trade. They let it be known that they wanted slaves, and would pay handsomely for them.

The Africans began by delivering their existing slaves. The Europeans wanted more. They guaranteed high profits to African suppliers who could give them enough slaves to satisfy their New World buyers. The Africans only knew one way to do this; they had to become slave hunters as well as slave sellers.

SOURCE DOCUMENT

. . . I was soon conducted to a prison, for three days, where I heard the groans and cries of many, and saw some of my fellow-captives. But when a vessel arrived to conduct us away to the ship, it was a most horrible scene; there was nothing to be heard but the rattling of chains, smacking of whips, and the groans and cries of our fellow-men. Some would not stir from the ground, when they were lashed and beat in the most horrible manner.[6]

Ottobah Cugoano, an enslaved African, wrote an account of the African slave trade that was published in 1787.

In the name of profit, they abandoned traditional practices and turned slavery into a business. African slave hunters staged raids, started wars, and sometimes grabbed people off the streets to fill their quotas. Whole villages fell victim to raiders who carried off many of the able-bodied adults.

European traders, always seeking ways to streamline operations, began building massive forts or "slave factories," as they were sometimes called. During the height of the slave trade, about sixty of these fortress-like structures dotted the coastline of western Africa. They served as collection points and secure holding facilities for captives awaiting shipment to New World slave markets.

The Middle Passage

When a loaded ship put to sea, the slaves faced the most brutal part of their long journey from freedom in Africa to slavery in America. They were chained together and packed like cordwood into dark and airless cargo holds.

A typical hold was perhaps five-feet, eight-inches deep, with closely spaced, six-foot-wide shelves built onto the walls. Slaves lay shoulder to shoulder on the floor. On the shelves, rows of three or even four people were crammed into the six-foot width. Lengthwise, the feet of each row touched the heads of the next.

In this way, four to six hundred people could be packed into the cargo space.

On average, one in five slaves would die before reaching the New World. They died of malnutrition; dysentery, smallpox, cholera, and other infectious diseases; or from brutal punishments for the smallest offenses. Some managed to kill themselves rather than face what lay ahead.

Captains expected slave deaths on every voyage, writing them off as just another cost of doing business. They were not so accepting of large or unusual losses that cut deeply into their profits.

While navigating the Middle Passage, slave ships held scores of slaves in their holds. The enslaved Africans had to deal with lack of food, cramped space, and very unsanitary conditions for months on end.

A slave named Zamba Zembola told of one such loss in his autobiography:

> . . . one evening, about sunset . . . a heavy squall struck the ship . . . laying her very nearly on her [side]. . . . The poor slaves below . . . [were thrown to one side], where they lay heaped on top of each other. . . . Fifteen of them were smothered or crushed to death, besides a great number who were cruelly bruised. The captain seemed [upset]; but [chiefly because of] the sudden loss of some five or six thousand dollars.[7]

In the New World

Slaves who made it to the New World often seemed more dead than alive. After weeks in a cargo hold on starvation rations, many were walking skeletons. They had bruises, open sores, and infections. Filth encrusted their bodies. Many could hardly walk.

The first order of business was getting the slaves ready to make a good showing. Most captains relied upon local slave merchants for this part of the job. The merchants fed the slaves, cleaned them up, and generally tried to make them look healthy and strong. Experienced dealers had a few tricks to get the look they wanted. For example, a rubdown with oil gave the dark skin of the Africans a sleek glow. Carefully applied paint could hide an injury or a blemish, and black hair dye could make graying slaves look younger.

While the merchant handled the sale, the captain began looking for a profitable return cargo. Sugar, coffee, molasses, tobacco, and other New World agricultural products were in high demand in Europe.

Like any business, the slave trade had its financial ups and downs. Some ships lost money or made scant profits. Some went down at sea and were never heard from again. Every losing expedition cut into overall profit percentages. Profits from successful expeditions had to cover these losses. The lore of the trade included a sprinkling of wildly profitable voyages. For example, the British slave ship *Lively* made a 300 percent profit in 1737.[8]

The American Trade

Drawn by these handsome profits, Americans began entering the slave trade in the early 1700s. Though the largest market for slaves was in the South, most American dealers operated out of Northern ports. This was largely because of economic differences between the two regions.

Commerce and industry shaped the Northern economy. It had the manufacturers to build and outfit the ships and an ambitious merchant class to underwrite the voyages. The South was overwhelmingly agricultural. Its sprawling plantations and isolated farms needed laborers who could do the backbreaking work of planting, tending, and harvesting the crops.

Thus, the South became a major market for slaves, while the North became a major supplier. Northern merchants sailed to Africa loaded with trade goods and returned with slaves for the Caribbean and the American South.

Tiny Rhode Island had the largest slaving operation in the colonies. The ports of Newport and Providence were well equipped to handle the comings and goings of an active trade. But geography was not the only reason the slave trade took hold in Rhode Island. It fit comfortably with the colony's principal industries: shipbuilding and rum distilling. Rhode Island shipbuilders became experts in the special needs of the slave trade. Rum distilleries were a ready market for molasses, a principal ingredient in rum. The rum was made from sugar cane from the South and the Caribbean and was sold in Europe.

At the same time that slavery was becoming a big business, the colonies crackled with talk of freedom from British rule. Freedom and slavery: dealing with these conflicting ideas would become an ongoing struggle for an infant nation founded upon principles of human equality.

2

FROM SERVANTS TO SLAVES

SLAVERY WAS NOT THE ONLY FORM OF UNFREE labor in colonial America. Indentured servitude was common until the transatlantic trade made slaves readily available. Indentured servants were usually poor whites looking for a new start in a new world. In return for passage and a place to stay, they sold themselves into servitude for a specified number of years. When the term ended, a servant was free to start a new life in the colonies.

The status of slaves was not as clear. They had no contracts to describe their duties or set time limits on their servitude. On the other hand, nothing in early colonial American law made slavery a lifelong condition that passed from parents to children.

Slaves for Life

The first known slave for life in the American colonies was a black man named John Punch.[1] In 1640, Punch and two white indentured servants ran away from their master's Virginia farm. They were caught in Maryland and hauled back to face charges. The judge ordered all three men flogged and sentenced the white runaways to four more years of servitude. He sentenced John Punch to "serve his said master . . . for the [rest] of his natural Life."[2]

This began the process that made American slavery into a permanent condition based upon race. As the institution grew, individual colonies began passing "slave codes." These were laws that regulated and controlled African-American life.

Virginia passed one of the first slave codes in 1705; it became a model for other colonies seeking to regulate their slaves. It began with a straightforward statement that "slaves within this dominion . . . shall be held to be real estate [property]."[3] It gave white masters complete control, even over life and death. According to the Virginia code, if a disobedient slave "shall happen to be killed [during] correction . . . the master shall be free of all punishment . . . as if such accident never happened."[4]

By 1750, slavery was legal in eleven of the thirteen original American colonies. However, it never developed

SOURCE DOCUMENT

All servants imported and brought into the Country. . . who were not Christians in their native Country. . . shall be accounted and be slaves. All Negro, mulatto and Indian slaves within this dominion. . . shall be held to be real estate. If any slave resists his master. . . correcting such slave, and shall happen to be killed in such correction. . . the master shall be free of all punishment. . . as if such accident never happened.[5]

With this Virginia General Assembly declaration in 1705, the enslavement of Africans had been firmly dictated by colonial law.

as fully in the North as it did in the South. Southern plantations grew labor-intensive crops such as rice, tobacco, sugar, and, later, cotton. With hundreds of acres under cultivation, planters needed a steady supply of cheap labor.

The Northern economy was based on trade and industry rather than agriculture. Its small-scale family farms did not depend upon slave labor. Neither did its factories. Industrialists found it easier and more profitable to use low-paid workers. They put in their ten to twelve hours and went home. The employer did not have to buy them from a slave trader or provide them with food, clothing, and housing.

Slavery in the North

Most Northern slaves worked as household servants or skilled tradesmen. They cleaned the house, cooked the meals, cared for children, and maintained the grounds. Because of this limited role, Northerners rarely owned large numbers of slaves. For example, the legendary abolitionist Sojourner Truth lived with five different owners in upstate New York. Most of them had no more than two or three slaves.

Truth was born in the late 1790s and sold away from her parents when she was just nine years old. She found herself the only slave of a childless but demanding couple. They expected her to work like an adult, constantly and hard. They made no allowances for her age or for the fact that she did not speak English.

Isabella, as Truth was first named, originally came from a Dutch-speaking household. Years later, she remembered what it was like with her next owners: "If they sent me for a frying-pan, not knowing what they meant, perhaps I carried them pot-hooks and trammels [devices for hanging cooking-kettles in fireplaces]. Then, oh! how angry mistress would be with me!"[6]

By the time Isabella came to live in this harsh

In this painting, Sojourner Truth reads with President Lincoln. Truth grew up a slave in New York and was not allowed to learn to read or write. However, she became a powerful speaker.

household, the state of New York had already sounded the death knell for slavery. The legislature established a plan of gradual emancipation in 1789. On July 4, 1827, all slaves born before 1799 became unconditionally free. Younger slaves became indentured servants for a time: until age twenty-eight for males and twenty-five for females.

The Roots of Southern Slavery

Slave owning planters dominated the political and social structure of Southern society. Like the nobles of the Middle Ages, they were aristocrats, secure in their standing at the top of the social pyramid. Beneath them were white tradesmen and small farmers, followed by poor whites who scratched out a living any way they could. Last of all came the slaves.

This class system almost crumbled in the 1780s. Economic woes threatened the entire plantation system and, with it, the institution of slavery. Falling prices and reduced demand for Southern crops left planters cash-strapped and desperate. Many of them began to think that they could no longer afford a year-round workforce of slaves.

There was open talk of emancipation. Some states passed laws to allow private manumission, the freeing of slaves by individual owners. With slavery fast disappearing in the North and now threatened in the South, it seemed on its way to extinction. Then, in 1793, inventor Eli Whitney presented his cotton gin to the world. The gin (short for "engine") did one job: separated the seeds and fibers of cotton. It could produce fifty pounds of cleaned cotton in the time it took a slave to handpick just one pound.

Before Eli Whitney's machine, Southern plantations produced around 1.5 million pounds of saleable cotton per year. By 1800, production shot up to 18 million pounds per year. It continued to increase as planters bought more land and more slaves so they could produce even more cotton. Thus, the machine that revolutionized an industry and saved an economy also preserved the institution of slavery, which would oppress millions of African Americans.

The Peculiar Institution

Growers were not the only ones who profited from King Cotton, as it came to be called. Northern textile mills manufactured raw cotton into cloth. Southern states that did not grow cotton sold slaves instead. North Carolina, Virginia, Maryland, and Delaware made a tidy profit, selling excess slaves to cotton growers in South Carolina and Georgia.

Thus, technology and slavery together shaped the cotton economy in the South. In the process, they made slavery into a permanent fixture of Southern life.

The invention of the cotton gin altered the southern economy so that cotton was a more important crop than tobacco, indigo, or rice.

It became known as the "peculiar institution," meaning that this form of slavery was like none other and belonged exclusively to the American South.

Southerners justified slavery with a combination of racism and paternalism ("father-like"). They claimed that blacks were inferior and could not take care of themselves. It fell to their white masters to care for them and protect them.

Masters spoke about "loving" their slaves and treating them as lesser members of a large extended family. For example, slave-owning Georgia minister Charles C. Jones encouraged masters to see to the spiritual needs of their slaves. To him, the obligation came not from human laws, but directly from God: "[Slaves] were placed under our control . . . not [only] for our benefit but for theirs also."[7]

Beyond Economics

Though the peculiar institution was rooted in economic necessity, its hold on the South went beyond dollars and cents. It shaped an entire culture. Slave codes gave owners near-total control of their human property, and made those enslaved more dependent upon their owners.

The reverse was also true; owners became dependent upon their slaves. This was especially true of the Southern elite, the handful of wealthy owners whose gracious, magnolias-and-lawn-parties world could not have existed without slave labor. Thus, any threat to the institution of slavery did not just endanger an economy. It endangered a way of life.

Southerners saw Northern abolition as a threat. Certainly, North and South were moving in opposite directions on the issue. By the end of the eighteenth century, the pattern was set. Slavery slowly disappeared in the North, yet thrived in the South. The conflict was economic, cultural, and political. It could rip the newborn nation apart if the two sides could not find common ground.

Slavery and the Founding Freedoms

We hold these Truths to be self-evident, that all Men are created equal, that they are endowed by their Creator with certain unalienable Rights, that among these are Life, Liberty, and the Pursuit of Happiness. . . . [1]

—Declaration of Independence
July 4, 1776

THIS STIRRING DECLARATION IS WIDELY regarded as one of the boldest statements of human rights ever written. It speaks of rights that cannot be taken away or even given away, and applies them equally to everyone.

In actual practice, "all men" did not include slaves or even free black people. Neither did the guarantees of the Constitution and the Bill of Rights. Some of the Founders considered this hypocritical. They questioned how a people could demand freedom for themselves while holding another people in slavery.

Ebenezer Hazard, a future Postmaster General of the United States, faced this hypocrisy head-on. In 1777, he made the following entry in his journal:

> It is astonishing that men who feel the value and importance of liberty . . . should keep such numbers of the human species in a state of . . . absolute [slavery]. Every argument which can be urged in favor of our own liberties will certainly operate with equal force in favor of that of the Negroes; nor can we . . . contend for the one while we withhold the other.[2]

Stirrings of Revolution

Before the Revolutionary War, the American colonists were subjects of the King of England. He could ignore their laws, limit their trade and commerce, and imposes taxes without their consent.

On September 5, 1774, the First Continental Congress assembled in Philadelphia. Within three weeks, the Congress hammered out an agreement called the "Continental Association," or simply the "Association." Its stated purpose was to "obtain redress of . . . grievances which threaten destruction to the lives, liberty, and property of his majesty's subjects in North America."[3]

To achieve this goal, the delegates soon decided "that a non-importation, non-consumption, and non-exportational agreement . . . will prove the most speedy, effectual, and peaceable measure."[4] In other words, the colonists would refuse to have any business dealings with Great Britain.

First on the boycott list were "goods, wares, or merchandise, as shall have been exported from Great-Britain or Ireland."[5] Next were slaves: "We will neither import nor purchase, any slave imported after the first day of Decem . . . next; after which time, we will wholly discontinue the slave trade . . . nor sell our commodities or manufactures to those who are concerned in it."[6]

Southerners accepted this clause as readily as Northerners. The boycott was a temporary measure; a political protest aimed at Great Britain. It was not a moral judgment against slavery.

The Declaration of Independence

Southerners did not accept Thomas Jefferson's first draft of the Declaration of Independence. It contained a paragraph that condemned the Atlantic slave trade in no uncertain terms. Jefferson accused the King of England of waging

> cruel war against human nature itself, violating it's [sic] most sacred rights of life and liberty in the persons of a distant people who never offended him, captivating & carrying them into slavery in another hemisphere, or to incur miserable death in their transportation [there].[7]

In an early draft of the Declaration of Independence, Thomas Jefferson included a passage that spoke out against King George III. The king had supported the slave trade, then wanted the slaves to fight against the rebels. Other patriots voted to take the passage out.

Jefferson's tone of moral reproach offended the Southern delegates. They feared that condemnation of the Atlantic trade would lead to condemnation of slavery itself. The South held firm, putting antislavery delegates into a difficult position. The Northerners knew that the revolution could not succeed unless all thirteen colonies stood united. They also knew that keeping Jefferson's paragraph would mean losing support in the South.

So the Founders cut Jefferson's paragraph from the Declaration. The final document mentions the words "free" and "independent" four times each. It mentions "rights" ten times. It does not mention "slavery" even once. Officially ignoring the issue allowed North and South to stand together against the British. It did not make the problem go away.

Thomas Jefferson's Dilemma

Thomas Jefferson grappled with the question of slavery all his adult life. The man who wrote those words about "life, liberty, and the pursuit of happiness" owned hundreds of slaves. In words much like those of Ebenezer Hazard, Jefferson expressed amazement that anyone "who would endure toil, famine . . . imprisonment & death itself [for] his own liberty [could] inflict on his fellow men a bondage, one hour of which is [filled] with more misery than ages of that [political injustice] he rose in rebellion to oppose."[8]

Despite his high-minded ideas, Thomas Jefferson contributed to the prejudices of his time. Though he condemned slavery in theory, he admitted to a suspicion "that the blacks . . . are inferior to the whites in the endowments both of body and mind. . . . [The] unfortunate difference of colour, and perhaps of [ability], is a powerful obstacle to the emancipation of these people."[9]

Because Jefferson considered black people inferior, he wanted to separate them from whites. He proposed emancipation, followed by resettlement. Freed slaves would be returned to Africa, or sent to some other place where they could have a homeland of their own.

As a young man, Jefferson had hoped that slavery would die a natural death. When this did not happen, he pulled back from the issue, both politically and personally. Jefferson never freed his own slaves. Even at his death, he did not let all of them go. His will freed only five; the others were sold along with the rest of his property.

No one knows why Thomas Jefferson behaved this way, or how he dealt with the conflict between his beliefs and his actions. He once came close to explaining in a letter to James Heaton of Ohio: "A good cause is often injured more by ill-timed efforts of its friends than by the arguments of its enemies . . . my [opinions] have been 40 years before the public. Had I repeated them 40 times, they would only have become the more stale and thread-bare."[10]

African Americans and the Revolution

In the time leading up to the Revolutionary War, freedom became an ideal, a demand, and finally a battle cry. Slaves became involved in the rebellion long before it turned into an actual war. The first American to fall in the conflict was a black man from Boston named Crispus Attucks.

It happened on March 5, 1770, when British soldiers fired into an unruly crowd of Americans. Attucks and four others died in what soon became known as the Boston Massacre. In a move that went against law and tradition, Crispus Attucks was buried in Park Street Cemetery along with the four white victims. All were honored as martyrs in the cause of liberty from British oppression.

Both slaves and free blacks fought at Bunker Hill on June 17, 1775. Though they fought well, George Washington decided to forbid the use of slaves as soldiers. This was a political rather than a military decision. Washington, himself a slave owner, understood Southern fears about arming slaves for any reason.

The British had no such fears. On November 7, 1775, Lord Dunmore, royal governor of the colony of Virginia, made an offer to black slaves and white indentured servants: "I do . . . declare all *indentured servants*, negroes, or others . . . *free*, that are able and willing to [join] . . . *his majesty's troops* . . ."[11] (Italics in source)

Slaves as Soldiers

As the war dragged on, the Continental Army was in constant need of troops. The idea of turning slaves into soldiers came up again. This time, it was sponsored by John Laurens, Jr., of South Carolina, a Southerner who opposed slavery on principle.

On January 14, 1778, he wrote to ask his father

> to cede [give] me a number of your able bodied men slaves . . . I would bring about a twofold good, first I would advance those who are unjustly deprived of the Rights of Mankind to a State which would be a proper [stage] between abject Slavery and perfect Liberty—and besides I would reinforce the Defenders of Liberty with a number of gallant Soldiers . . .[12]

In March of 1779, Alexander Hamilton recommended raising battalions of black soldiers under the command of John Laurens, Jr.:[13]

> I have not the least doubt that the negroes will make very excellent soldiers, with proper management . . .

I frequently hear [the objection that negroes] are too stupid to make soldiers . . . I think their want of cultivation (for their natural faculties are probably as good as ours) joined to that habit of subordination which they acquire from a life of servitude, will make them sooner become soldiers than our White inhabitants.[14]

SOURCE DOCUMENT

. . . many Negroes and Mulattoes . . . have concealed themselves on board the Ships in the harbor; that some still continue to attach themselves to British Officers and that others have attempted to impose themselves upon the officers of the French and American Armies as Freemen and to make their escapes in that manner, In order to prevent their succeeding in such practices All Officers . . . are directed not to suffer any such negroes or mulattoes to be retained in their Service but . . . to cause them to be delivered to the Guards . . . Mr. David Ross will have the superintendency and will give passes to enable them to return to their Masters . . .[15]

On October 25, 1781, George Washington gave orders to ensure that slaves who fought in the Revolutionary War were returned to slavery. Washington was a slave owner himself.

In time, deaths and widespread desertions threatened to undermine the revolution. George Washington and other leaders saw no choice; they had to allow African Americans into the Continental Army. By the end of the war, some five thousand African Americans had served. Though some soldiers did earn their freedom, the overall plight of blacks did not change. White prejudice continued, and so did the institution of slavery.

The Articles of Confederation

When the Second Continental Congress met to form a new government, delegates argued openly about slavery. On November 15, 1777, they passed the Articles of Confederation. The document itself said nothing about slavery or the status of blacks. It focused on the rights, privileges, and duties of whites.

Slavery became an issue when Congress tried to establish a basis for taxes. Everyone agreed that the states should pay expenses for the national government. The problem was distributing the financial burden. Coping with this problem raised an old and troubling question: Were slaves persons or property?

The first draft of the articles based taxes upon each state's total population. Samuel Chase of Maryland had a different idea. He wanted to count the white population only. Slaves were simply property, Chase

Samuel Chase felt that enslaved African Americans should be treated like property.

claimed: "negroes . . . should not be considered as members of the state [any] more than cattle."[16]

On August 1, 1776, the Chase amendment failed to pass Congress. The delegates went back to work, hammering out a compromise that based taxation upon the value of a state's land and improvements. Other types of property—including slaves—did not figure into the count. Thus, Congress bypassed slavery as it had done with the Declaration of Independence. In the political climate of the time, delegates on both sides believed that this was the only way to reach a working agreement.

Even with the compromises, the Articles of Confederation faced a rough road through the various state legislatures. Not until March 1, 1781 did they officially become the law of the land. Less than nine months later, on October 19, 1781, British commander Lord Charles Cornwallis surrendered to General George Washington of the Continental Army. The Americans had defeated the most powerful empire in the world. The United States was free to begin its experiment in democracy.

CHAPTER 4

COMPROMISE AND THE CONSTITUTION

AFTER THE AMERICAN REVOLUTION, THE newborn nation soon outgrew the Articles of Confederation. Laws that made sense on paper were not effective in practice. It became clear that the articles needed major revisions.

One of the first calls for change focused on federal revenue. Using land value to determine each state's share of national expenses was proving to be both unfair and unworkable.

The Three-Fifths Compromise

In 1783, a committee led by Massachusetts representative Nathaniel Gorham went back to the idea of basing a state's share of federal expenses on its population. This would require an amendment to the Articles of Confederation. The proposed amendment would have to pass Congress and then go to the states for ratification.

It would be a long and difficult process. Every member of Congress realized that no amendment would succeed without substantial compromise. The South would never agree to include slaves in its population figures, nor would the North agree to count only whites.

Congress leaned toward a compromise that would count a percentage of a state's slaves in its population figures. But what percentage would be acceptable to both sides?

The committee working on the issue proposed counting two slaves as one freeman. In other words, half of the slaves would count in the general population. The South found that acceptable. The North did not. In a lengthy debate, several different percentages were proposed and rejected.

Finally, James Madison suggested a ratio of five–to–three: five slaves would count as three freeman. This was the famous three-fifths compromise or "federal ratio," as many people called it. Congress passed the amendment on April 18, 1783, and sent it to the states for ratification. Four states refused to ratify, and so the amendment never became part of the Articles of Confederation.

The Constitutional Convention

On May 25, 1787, the Constitutional Convention opened at Independence Hall in Philadelphia. The delegates originally planned to revise and extend the Articles of Confederation. George Reed of Delaware was one of the first to realize that reworking the articles would not be enough.

According to James Madison's notes, Reed

> was against patching up the old federal system. . . . The Confederation was founded on temporary principles. It cannot last; it cannot be amended. If we do not establish a good government on new principles, we must either go to ruin or have the work to do over again.[1]

Most of the other delegates agreed, and so they set to work. At the beginning sessions they discussed procedures and goals. Then, on May 29,

James Madison is known as the "Father of the Constitution." He was the driving force behind the convention and kept a thorough journal of the proceedings. He also proposed the three-fifths compromise to quiet the debate over slavery.

they got down to the business of creating a legislature, or lawmaking body, for the new nation.

Creating the Legislature

The task of designing a legislative body raised many questions. Should the legislature have one house or two? How many legislators should represent each state? Should representation be equal or proportional?

Small states generally wanted equal representation, with each state having the same number of legislators. The larger states favored proportional representation, with the number of legislators based upon the number of people in each state.

On the first full day of deliberations, Governor Edmund Randolph of Virginia presented his state's plan. It provided for a bicameral, or two-house, legislature. The first branch would be elected by the people, and those representatives would then choose members of the second branch. According to Randolph, both branches would have proportional representation, based on "the Quotas of contribution [taxes paid into the federal treasury], [or] the number of free inhabitants, as the one or the other rule may seem best in different cases."[2]

The mention of proportional representation plunged the convention into a familiar argument about counting slaves. Southern states wanted to boost their representation in Congress by including slaves in the population. In some states, this could make a huge difference. For example, 43 percent of South Carolina's population was enslaved (107,094 slaves out of a total population of 249,073).[3] Assuming one representative for every 30,000 people, South Carolina would have 83 representatives if all slaves were counted. If none of the slaves were counted, the number of representatives would drop to 47.

The Great Compromise

The struggle over organizing a national legislature almost tore the Constitutional Convention apart. Then, Roger Sherman of Connecticut proposed a compromise. Congress would have two branches: one with equal representation by state, the other with proportional representation based on the free population of each state. Sherman's idea of a balanced, two house, legislature gave each side something it wanted. However, the slave states would never agree to it if they could not count their slaves.

James Wilson of Pennsylvania, who would later serve on the first Supreme Court, was a determined opponent of slavery. He was also a politician, who understood that compromise was necessary to the political process. Wilson proposed using the three-fifths rule or "federal ratio." Three out of five slaves would count toward a state's population. This would mean that South Carolina could count 64,257 of its 107,094 slaves toward its population.

The North insisted that if three-fifths of the slave population counted toward representation, the same proportion should also count toward taxation. The South reluctantly agreed.

Having worked out the terms of the compromise, many delegates did not want to discuss slavery in the founding document of a free nation. Congress therefore replaced the word with a less offensive term:

> Representatives and direct taxes shall be apportioned among the several states . . . according to their . . . numbers, which shall be determined by adding to the whole number of free persons, including those bound to service for a term of years [indentured servants] and . . . three fifths of all other Persons.[4]

Antislavery people could take some comfort from the language of the compromise. At least it acknowledged slaves as "persons" rather than just property. Some Southerners found that concept threatening. Others believed that it presented their peculiar institution more truthfully. James Madison, the Virginia slave owner known as the father of the Constitution, explained his view:

> We must deny the fact that slaves are considered merely as property, and in no [way] whatsoever as persons. The

true state of the case is, that they partake of both these qualities; being considered by our laws, in some [ways] as persons, and in other [ways], as property.[5]

Slave owners were not satisfied with gaining seats in a house of representatives. They wanted other protections for their peculiar institution. For example, South Carolina and Georgia led an effort to preserve the triangle trade. They also pressed for a fugitive slave

Much like at this slave auction in New Orleans, Louisiana, slaves were bought and sold like property. Slave traders often forced slaves to smile, so that they would be more appealing to prospective buyers.

law so escaping slaves would have no safe haven in the United States.

American Slavery and the International Trade

By the time of the Constitutional Convention, the horrors of the Middle Passage were well known. Everyone had heard the accounts of filthy cargo holds, epidemic diseases, and unwanted slaves thrown alive into the sea. Many Southerners sincerely despised these brutalities. Some of them considered the transatlantic trade a necessary evil.

In the upper South, a good number of people wanted the trade to end. Its disgraceful record reflected badly upon them, and in their view, upon the peculiar institution itself. Those Southerners who held this view found themselves in league with Northern antislavery advocates.

In another odd partnership, plantation owners in the Deep South and ship owners in New England found themselves on the same side. Both stood to benefit by saving the trade. South Carolina and Georgia wanted a continuing supply of slaves to work their vast cotton plantations. The New England traders wanted to save a profitable business.

For a time, it seemed that these issues would tie up the convention in endless debate. Then South Carolina and Georgia further complicated the process by taking a bold step. They refused to ratify a constitution that abolished the slave trade.

This put the debate on a different level. It became a devil's choice, or a choice between two evils. Antislavery delegates had to choose between allowing a practice they despised, or letting the union collapse. With the future of the nation at stake, they looked for a third alternative, a compromise that both sides could accept. The best they could do was to avoid the problem by pushing it twenty years into the future.

Denying Safe Haven to Runaway Slaves

With the question of the transatlantic trade settled, South Carolina and Georgia moved on to their next issue: runaway slaves. With no national policy, each state made up its own rules. A slave could become free simply by taking refuge in a state that banned slavery. The Southern delegations wanted to change that.

On August 28, 1787, South Carolina moved that a fugitive slave clause be added to the Constitution. In round about language, this clause protected property rights of slave owners without once mentioning the institution of slavery:

> "No Person held to Service or labor in one State . . . [who escapes] into another, shall . . . be discharged from such service or labour, but shall be delivered [to] the party to whom such service or labour may be due."[6]

The Struggle for Ratification

On September 17, 1787, the final draft of the Constitution went to Congress. Convention delegates returned home to champion the cause of ratification in their state legislatures. They needed nine states to ratify the Constitution before it could become the law of the land.

Some who supported the Constitution made a point of reaching out to the general public as well as state officials. For example, John Jay, Alexander Hamilton, and James Madison wrote *The Federalist* papers under the pen name, Publius. Point by point, these eighty-five essays made the case for the ratification of the Constitution.

Though the writers shared a common distaste for slavery, it did not become a major issue in *The Federalist Papers*. Numbers 38 and 42 mention it briefly; only Number 54 discusses it in any detail. All three of these essays are attributed to James Madison.

At the convention, Madison managed to sidestep the slavery issue. He could not do that when he presented the Constitution to the Virginia state legislature. As a Virginian himself, and a slave owner, Madison had expected close questioning on anything to do with slavery. He assured the slave-owning legislators that the fugitive slave clause would protect their property rights: "At present, if any slave [goes] to any of those states where slaves are free, he becomes [free] by their laws . . . This [new] clause [allows] owners of slaves to reclaim them. This is better security than any that now exists."[7]

Madison's approach broke down one of the last barriers to ratification. On June 21, 1788, the Constitution became law. Slavery was an unnamed, yet very real, presence in this testament to freedom. The Constitution had secured the international trade for another twenty years, counted more than half the slave population towards seats in the House of Representatives, and left runaway slaves with little hope for a safe haven.

This happened in spite of the fact that slavery was fast disappearing in the North. It happened because the political process in a democracy works through compromise. That fact would become clearer as Americans continued to deal with slavery in a nation dedicated to freedom and equality.

5

SLAVERY IN A GROWING NATION

AFTER THE REVOLUTIONARY WAR, THE UNITED States pushed westward, opening new territories, creating new states. Disputes over slavery became commonplace during this expansion. The disagreements usually came down to the same thing; the South wanted to spread slavery into new territories and the North wanted to keep it out.

Both sides were looking to the future. Northerners wanted to keep slavery from spreading so it could eventually be destroyed. Southerners wanted it to grow and become such a part of national life that it could not be banned or even restricted. For many in the South, their economy and their way of life depended upon the peculiar institution.

The Northwest Ordinance

The Constitutional Convention was still in session when Congress passed the Northwest Ordinance on July 13, 1787. It was the last major legislation passed under the Articles of Confederation.

The ordinance applied to the territory east of the Mississippi River and north of the Ohio River. It laid out a detailed plan for forming "not less than three nor more than five" states in the region.[1] These states would not be colonies with limited rights of self-government. They would be equals in every way to the original thirteen states.

To people who just fought a war over being ruled by a faraway empire, this assurance meant a great deal. Settlers poured into the region. In time, they would create the states of Ohio, Indiana, Illinois, Michigan, and Wisconsin.

Massachusetts lawyer Nathan Dane drafted the final version of the Northwest Ordinance. When it came before Congress on July 11, it did not mention slavery at all. Dane proposed that it should, and presented article six to Congress. It was a straightforward statement that not only banned slavery, but actually used the word: "There shall be neither slavery nor involuntary servitude in the said territory, otherwise than in the punishment of crimes, whereof the party shall have been duly convicted."[2]

THE NORTHWEST TERRITORY was divided into the five following states (with Minnesota east of the Mississippi): 1. Ohio, admitted 1803; 2. Indiana, admitted 1816; 3. Illinois, admitted 1818; 4. Michigan, admitted 1837; 5. Wisconsin, admitted 1848. (See note on map of U. S. 1783.)

THE
NORTHWEST TERRITORY, 1787
South Carolina ceded her western
territory to the U. S. in 1787

SCALE OF MILES
0 50 100 200 300 400

Longitude   West   from   82   Greenwich   77

Slavery was banned in the Northwest Territory.

A fugitive slave clause followed, but even that did not destroy the importance of this article. A major piece of legislation had called slavery by name and banned it from an entire region.

Even more surprising, the Southern states did not object. They joined in what became a unanimous vote for the measure. Historians and other scholars have long wondered why they did this.

Some suggest that Southern congressmen may have decided that slavery simply would not take root in the North. It was already disappearing in the original states of the Northeast. There was no reason to believe that the new states of the Northwest would be any different.

Whatever the reasons, the Northwest Ordinance created a territory that would never know legalized slavery. This alone seemed to hold promise for the future of freedom.

The Bill of Rights

The Northwest Ordinance and the Constitution both went before Congress in the summer of 1787. This fact alone probably led to comparisons and contrasts. The most obvious difference was that the ordinance banned slavery while the Constitution did not.

The Northwest Ordinance also contained guarantees of individual rights such as freedom of religion, trial by jury, and protection against "cruel or unusual punishment."[3] The Constitution did not. Many of America's Founders considered this a mistake.

Slavery was not an issue in the debate on the Bill of Rights. Congress did not wrestle with the persons-versus-property question, nor argue about which amendments applied to slaves and which did not. There was no need. The Bill of Rights, passed in 1788, described the rights of free people living in a free society. By definition, it did not apply to slaves.

This was understood by all concerned, but never mentioned. Everyone knew that any attempt to discuss the rights of slaves would doom the Bill of Rights before it could be drafted.

Slavery was mentioned only once, in the remarks of South Carolina representative Charles Pinckney. He cited the fact of slavery as a reason for opposing the addition of a Bill of Rights: "such bills generally begin with declaring that all men are by nature born free." Pinckney claimed that such a declaration would be meaningless "when a large part of our property consists [of] men who are actually born slaves."[4]

Perhaps Pinckney made his case, for the Bill of Rights did not begin with a soaring testimony to freedom and equality. It began with only a brief and matter-of-fact introduction: "ARTICLES IN Addition to, and Amendment of, the Constitution of the United

States of America, proposed by Congress, and ratified by the Legislatures of the several States . . . "[5]

Defining "The People"

The Bill of Rights did not change the Constitution. It simply applied constitutional principles to individual liberties. It said nothing about who was, and who was not, entitled to these liberties. That had already been done in the body of the Constitution.

Its opening words—"We the people"—did not mean everyone who lived in the United States. The framers divided the population into three groups: free white people (including indentured servants), American Indians, and "other persons" (slaves).

Only members of the first group belonged to "the people." American Indians did not qualify because they lived separately and governed themselves. Enslaved African Americans did not qualify because they were neither free nor white.

In 1790, Congress went one step further in defining "the people." It passed a law limiting citizenship to white immigrants. Race had always been a factor in the slave trade, but the Immigration Act of 1790 strengthened it. The United States government had officially linked race and citizenship.

This came at a time when the division between slave and free states was becoming a fact of American political life. The famous Mason-Dixon Line divided the states geographically. Slavery divided them politically and economically. It was banned in the seven Northern states—Pennsylvania, Massachusetts, Rhode Island, Connecticut, New York, New Hampshire, and New Jersey. It had become a way of life in the six states of the South—Maryland, Delaware, Virginia, North Carolina, South Carolina, and Georgia.

A Slave Named John

In 1793, a dispute over the fate of one man made the recapture of runaway slaves a national problem. It started ten years earlier, when a slave named John was declared free under Pennsylvania law. John's owner did not accept that ruling. Instead of obeying it, he hired John out to a planter in Virginia.

After five more years of slavery, John escaped and returned to Pennsylvania. His second experience of freedom ended when three slave catchers tracked him down and took him back to Virginia.

The Pennsylvania Abolition Society took John's case to Governor Thomas Mifflin. They pointed out that John was free under Pennsylvania law. In their minds, that made his "recapture" a kidnapping and the three slave catchers, kidnappers.

Governor Mifflin wrote to Virginia governor Beverley Randolph. He asked that the kidnappers be returned to Pennsylvania for trial, and that John be restored to freedom. When Randolph refused, Mifflin sought help from an old comrade-in-arms: President George Washington. Washington turned the problem over to Attorney General Edmund Randolph, who put it before Congress.

The Fugitive Slave Act of 1793

In November 1792, a Senate committee met to draft a bill relating to "fugitives from justice, and persons escaping from the service of their masters."[6] The result was the Fugitive Slave Act of 1793, which President Washington signed into law on February 12.

Actually, the law was not entirely about runaway slaves. The first two sections dealt with fugitives from justice: criminals or accused criminals who tried to outrun the law by going to another state. The third dealt with runaway slaves. The fourth and final section set a fine of five hundred dollars for helping or hiding a fugitive.

The new law met opposition from many quarters. Officials in free states resented being turned into slave catchers for Southern planters. Opponents of slavery stood ready to defy the law if they could not find a way around it.

Slaves looking for a safe haven were not the only ones hurt by the Fugitive Slave Law. Free blacks also

Runaway slaves were always in danger of being returned to slavery, especially after the Fugitive Slave Law of 1793 was passed.

lived in fear of it. In the South, people assumed that every African American was a slave unless he or she could prove otherwise. Slave catchers carried that attitude with them when they pursued fugitives into the free states of the North.

Slavery and the Louisiana Purchase

A decade after the Fugitive Slave Act became law, President Thomas Jefferson made a key real estate deal. On April 30, 1803, he bought the Louisiana territory from France for $15 million.

The purchase immediately doubled America's size, adding about eight hundred thousand square miles of land. The territory stretched from the Mississippi River to the Rocky Mountains and from Canada down to the Gulf of Mexico. It was mostly untamed wilderness, with settlement limited to the southern region. Europeans had created a plantation economy, complete with wealthy landowners, sprawling fields, and black slaves to tend the crops.

Because slavery had a foothold in Louisiana, the United States government decided to leave it alone. This approach became a national policy for new states and territories. In places where slavery already existed, the government allowed it to continue. To do otherwise might mean facing a battle that very few politicians wanted to fight.

Congressional opponents of slavery could do little more than keep it in check. They worked to stop it from spreading into new areas and to maintain an uneasy balance of power between slavery and anti-slavery factions in Congress.

The Economy and the Triangle Trade

One area of agreement between these factions was the international slave trade. In the years since the Constitutional Convention, North and South had come to realize that the trade should be banned. While moral reasons were a factor, so were economic ones.

An end to the African trade would increase the cost of existing slaves. For owners, this meant an increase in property values. For sellers, it meant higher prices for their human merchandise. This was especially important in the upper South, where many planters faced failing crops and falling prices for their indigo, an ingredient in dyes, and tobacco. Eliminating competition from Africa would create a stronger—and more profitable—market for their own surplus slaves. Some planters could earn more selling their slaves than selling their crops.

Despite rising feelings against the trade, Congress could not end it until 1808, the year specified in the Constitution. In the meantime, the states placed their own embargoes on the "horrid traffic," as one Pennsylvania clergyman called it.[7] But a patchwork of often conflicting laws made enforcement difficult, if not impossible.

The States and the Triangle Trade

In 1803, a majority of Congress decided to strengthen the non-slave states' position. On February 28, it passed a new law with a cumbersome title: "An Act to Prevent the Importation of Certain Persons into Certain States, Where, by the Laws Thereof, Their Admission is Prohibited."

Basically, this act made breaking state laws against the slave trade a federal crime. The punishment for breaking this law was a fine of one thousand dollars for "any negro, mulatto, or other person of colour" illegally brought into a state.[8] That would be equal to more than twelve thousand dollars today.

The law did not sit well with many South Carolinians. Even those who opposed the trade often resented federal involvement in state affairs. They were even more resentful when an enthusiastic customs collector actually tried to enforce the law. James Simons impounded a slave ship that had just offloaded its human cargo at Charleston harbor.

Concern over federal intrusion into state business may have been partly responsible for South Carolina repealing its ban on the international slave trade in 1803. The trade had been banned in South Carolina since the Revolutionary War. By repealing the law, they left the federal government with no justification for becoming involved in South Carolina politics.

The End of the Legal Trade

People around the country, and especially in the South, were outraged by South Carolina's action. Repealing the ban on the international slave trade after sixteen years appeared to be a step backwards. It made opponents of the trade all the more eager to end it once and for all.

Several state legislatures discussed amending the Constitution so Congress could act immediately. That

SOURCE DOCUMENT

Let the first of January, the day of the abolition of the slave trade in our country, be set apart in every year, as a day of publick thanksgiving for that mercy. Let the history of the sufferings of our brethren, and of their deliverance, descend by this means to our children, to the remotest generations; and when they shall ask, in time to come, saying, What mean the lessons, the psalms, the prayers and the praises in the worship of this day? let us answer them, by saying, the Lord, on the day of which this is the anniversary, abolished the trade . . . [9]

Reverend Absalom Jones, African-American cofounder of Philadelphia's African Methodist Episcopal Church delivered a sermon on the banning of the slave trade.

idea never gained widespread support, but it did suggest a less extreme measure: passing the law ahead of time, so it would be ready to go into effect at the first possible moment. In December 1806, President Thomas Jefferson called upon Congress to do exactly that. Deliberations started within days. On March 2, 1807, Jefferson signed the bill into law. It would automatically become effective on January 1, 1808.

The end of the legal slave trade in the United States did not put an end to the capture and transport of Africans. For years afterward, some Americans would risk their lives and fortunes to traffic illegally in slaves. In addition, the trade continued legally in nations such as France, Spain, and Portugal.

Outlawing the international trade did not change the lives of American slaves. The new law carefully avoided any statement about domestic slavery. That was the price for Southern cooperation. Strictly limiting the law to the international trade allowed North and South to work together.

6

MISSOURI AND THE WESTWARD EXPANSION

CONFLICTS ABOUT SLAVERY CONTINUED TO be an issue as the nation spread westward. The addition of each new territory or state triggered a power struggle between slavery and antislavery factions. Both sides realized that expansion was the key to long-term survival for the peculiar institution. Therefore, Northern antislavery advocates wanted to hold slavery in check, while Southern slave owners wanted to spread it into new territories.

This conflict of ideas was built into the political and economic realities of the time. It could not be solved by persuading one side or the other to change its position. Both North and South held firm. Only a series of political compromises kept the national government from becoming paralyzed over the issue of slavery in the West.

The Missouri Question

The first of those compromises began in 1819, when Congress was considering Missouri's petition for statehood. Because the Missouri Territory already had slaves, many people took it for granted that it would become a slave state.

Then, on February 13, 1819, Congressman James Tallmadge of New York proposed an amendment to the bill authorizing Missouri statehood. It amounted to a plan for the gradual abolition of slavery in Missouri. The amendment did not affect slaves already in Missouri, but it prohibited owners from transporting new slaves into the state. It further provided that those born to Missouri slaves should be freed at the age of twenty-five.

Tallmadge expected objections, but he was not prepared for the fury of Southern reactions. One Southern representative said "that, if we persist, the Union will be dissolved" and claimed that opponents of slavery had "kindled a fire which all the waters of the ocean cannot put out, which [only] seas of blood can . . . [extinguish]."[1]

This was one of the first public threats of secession (disunion, or separation from) the United States. It forced both sides to realize how deep the gulf between them had become.

The Southern Defense

Missouri's hopes for statehood almost got lost in the angry debates over the single issue of slavery. The two sides approached it from completely different viewpoints. Northerners saw slavery as a moral issue. Southerners did not. To them, slavery was a necessity.

In their world, slavery of the "inferior" black race was part of the natural order. According to Charles Pinckney of South Carolina, Southern slaves were well treated and generally content: "Being without education, and born to obey . . . they are happier than they can possibly be if free,"[2]

He later shifted his focus to economic issues: "Have the Northern States any idea of the value of our slaves? At least, sir, six hundred millions of dollars. If we lose them, the value of the lands they cultivate will be [lowered] . . . and an annual income of at least forty millions of dollars will be lost . . ."[3] Pinckney closed with a threat that opposition to slavery could lead to "the division of this Union and a civil war."[4]

When both sides had stated their cases, Congress stalled on the Missouri question. It was clear that neither side could win over the other. The only hope short of war was a political solution, a compromise that made sense to both sides.

Finding such a compromise would not be easy. The South would not accept a ban on slavery in Missouri. The North would never agree to upset the balance of the Senate. At the time, each side had eleven states, represented by twenty-two senators. Adding Missouri as a twelfth slave state would give the South twenty-four Senators.

The Forces of Compromise

The possibilities for compromise brightened when Maine applied for statehood in December 1819. Speaker of the House Henry Clay and others decided to link Maine's application to Missouri's. Maine would enter the Union as a free state, Missouri as a slave state. This would maintain the balance of the Senate.

Northerners still objected to allowing slavery into any part of the Louisiana Territory. They wanted the American West to become "free soil," where slavery would never be permitted. The solution came from the Senate. Jesse B. Thomas of Illinois proposed dividing the territory geographically at 36°30' north latitude. North of that line, only Missouri would have slavery. South of it, new states could decide the issue for themselves.

Senator Thomas put the proposal together and

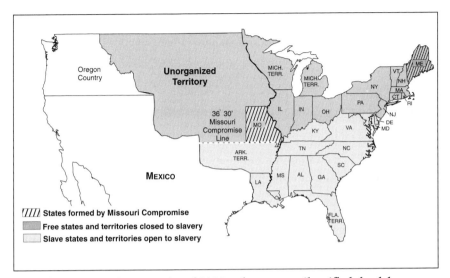

The Missouri Compromise of 1820 only temporarily stifled the debate over slavery.

Henry Clay shepherded it through Congress. Clay had a politician's gift for compromise and he used it well. In the process, he earned his nickname—"the Great Compromiser." It would follow him for the rest of his public career.

True to Clay's compromise, Maine became the twenty-third state in the Union on March 15, 1820. Missouri began drafting a state constitution with no restrictions on slavery. On August 10, 1821, Missouri took its place among the states.

The Missouri Compromise avoided a crisis that could have destroyed the Union. It also set policies for the future. For thirty years, new states would be admitted to the Union in pairs: one slave, and one free. The 36°30' line became a recognized border, dividing free North from slave South.

The Hidden Costs of the Missouri Compromise

Though the compromise reduced confrontations between North and South, some of its backers had second thoughts. It was at best a short-term solution to a long-term problem.

Thomas Jefferson, retired by this time and living in Virginia, never supported the compromise. In a letter to Massachusetts Congressman John Holmes, he wrote that "this momentous question, like a firebell in the night, awakened and filled me with terror. I considered it . . . the [death] knell of the Union. It is hushed, indeed, for the moment. But this is a [postponement] only, not a final sentence."[5]

It was not the pairing of slave and free states that bothered Jefferson. It was the "geographical line" which divided North and South for "moral and political" reasons. That line, said Jefferson, "will never be [completely removed]; and every new irritation will mark it deeper and deeper."[6]

Jefferson was right about the line. It became a constant reminder of the division between North and South. Some Southerners began to think that it might just as well be a border between sovereign, or self-governing, nations. The South was still a long way from secession, but the seed had been planted. It was an idea that would not go away.

Redefining Freedom and Slavery in the South

The Missouri crisis forced the South to deal with an old and troubling problem: justifying slavery in a nation that, according to the Declaration of Independence, was dedicated to the freedom and equality of "all men." For years, politicians had worked around the issue. They put whites and blacks into different categories without defining what those categories really meant.

During the decade after the Missouri crisis, Southerners firmed up their position. Most decided that the Declaration of Independence did not proclaim universal human rights. They felt its guarantees applied to whites only.

Some Southerners claimed that black slavery was morally acceptable because it was necessary to white freedom. Slave labor allowed the Southern "aristocracy" to be a leisure class. Actually working for a living was beneath them. They expected to live off their lands and family fortunes, while slaves did the menial tasks necessary for their owners' comfort.

A society based on slavery did not lend itself to a robust and varied economy. Tradition counted more than ambition, so life moved slowly in the South. The slaves worked, and the masters busied themselves with what they called "the finer things of life."

Southern dislike for Northern mercantilism, or emphasis on trade and industry, reached all levels of society. Southern aristocrats looked down on Northern industrialists. Even the poorest of white hardscrabble farmers looked down on the equally poor factory workers of the North.

The North and the Market Economy

In the early nineteenth century, economic differences between North and South became more pronounced. The industrialized North developed a market economy, while "King Cotton" transformed the South.

In the North, new technologies in transportation and communication helped to shape the market economy. Steamboats carried cargo and passengers on rivers and through manmade canals. Railroads operated over inland routes, connecting cities, towns, and out-of-the-way farmsteads. Later, Samuel Morse's telegraph allowed rapid communication between distant points.

These technologies reshaped the workplace, gradually replacing the household economy of earlier times. For generations, family units had grown their own food, made their own clothes, and even built

Northern factory workers put in long days for starvation wages. Poverty was a fact of life for workers like these women, shown weaving cloth on giant looms.

their own houses. Craftsmen and shopkeepers took pride in owning their businesses "lock, stock, and barrel." Except for young people starting out in life, working for someone else was a sign of failure.

The market economy changed those rules. Thousands of Americans gave up some of their independence for steady wages. In the process, they became consumers rather than producers; buying what they needed instead of making it at home. This produced a demand for more products and thus created more jobs.

So the cycle of earning and spending continued, at

least for the middle and upper classes. The poor were reduced to menial, low-paying factory jobs. They worked long hours, yet earned barely enough to pay for the necessities of life.

Some of these "wage slaves," as they were sometimes called, might have been as poor as actual slaves on a Southern plantation. However, their employers did not own them. They were free to seek better-paying and more satisfying jobs elsewhere.

The South and the Cotton Economy

The North had a diversified, or varied, economy. This meant that prosperity did not depend upon any single business or industry. That was not true in the South, especially after the rise of King Cotton.

The cotton plantations thrived because they offered the right product at the right time. Textile, or cloth, manufacturing had become important in the North and also in Europe. There, mills bought raw cotton as fast as the plantations could produce it.

To keep up with demand, cotton growers bought more and more slaves, mostly from the upper South. This caused an enormous shift in African-American population patterns. By the middle of the nineteenth century, about 1.8 million of the South's 2.5 million slaves lived and worked in the cotton states of the Deep South.[7]

The Southern economy was supported mainly by cotton. The use of slave labor boosted profits for many plantation owners.

Their labor made the plantations profitable, but not economically independent. The cotton states needed the upper South for slaves, and the North for business services such as insurance, transport, and marketing. Because of this dependence, a poor harvest or a drop in prices for raw cotton could devastate the Southern economy.

Likewise, anything that threatened slavery was cause for alarm. Protecting that institution was a matter

SOURCE DOCUMENT

The great enemy of the white man in these regions is the climate—no white man can ever work with impunity in this climate—no race but the African can ever stand the burning heat and fatal miasmas [atmospheres] of the Rice fields, and of the Cotton fields; and it is worthy of note that the first attempt to establish African slavery in Georgia, originated in this section of the State—and especially worthy of note that the reasons which led the citizens of Savannah and the surrounding country, to petition the Trustees of the colony of Georgia, to introduce negroes, still exists, in spite of the ravings of dishonest abolitionism.[8]

Joseph Jones, a scientist and professor from Georgia, tried to justify slavery by saying that only African Americans were fit to work in hot weather. In reality, it can be dangerous for all people to work in hot weather.

of economic survival to many Southerners. At even the suspicion of a threat to slavery, Southerners closed ranks. This partly explains the bitterness of the debate over the Missouri Compromise of 1820.

In that confrontation, Northerners tended to see a moral issue. Southerners saw a threat to their social, political, and economic survival. The compromise restored order and opened the way west for both sides. It allowed slavery and antislavery people to work together for a time, but it could not truly unify them.

The issue of slavery had created a gulf between North and South. Many people feared that it would grow until the Missouri Compromise would not be enough to bridge it.

CHAPTER 7

SLAVERY AND MANIFEST DESTINY

THE 1840S WERE A TIME OF EXPLOSIVE GROWTH. Between the beginning of the Mexican War in 1846 and California statehood in 1850, the United States added more than a million square miles of territory. The nation stretched across the broad middle of North America, from the Atlantic Ocean in the east to the Pacific in the west. Many believed that this was America's "manifest destiny," to tame a continent and become a great empire.

The Dream of Empire

The term "manifest destiny" did not exist when James K. Polk ran for President in 1844. However, the idea behind it most certainly did. Polk was an outspoken expansionist. He based his campaign on "the rean-nexation of Texas and the reoccupation of Oregon."[1]

Congress had already turned down a Texas request for statehood because Northerners did not want to admit another slave state. The Oregon Country, as it was called, had no slaves. By linking the two, Polk hoped to unite North and South behind his candidacy and also promote the cause of American expansion.

Polk's dream of taking over the Pacific Northwest led to one of the most famous campaign slogans in American history: "fifty-four forty or fight." Fifty-four forty referred to the latitude of the Oregon country's northern border. At that time, the Oregon territory included a good part of what is now western Canada, as well as the present states of Washington, Oregon, and Idaho, along with parts of Montana and Wyoming.

James K. Polk worked to expand the United States. The acquisition of this additional territory fueled the political battle over slavery.

The slogan implied that Polk would fight for Oregon if necessary. That made for good speeches and campaign slogans. It did not make good foreign policy. The last thing the United States needed was a war over Oregon, especially when a war over Texas loomed as a real possibility.

Though Texas had won independence from Mexico in 1836, strong political and economic ties remained, at least on the part of the Mexicans. United States interference with those ties might well lead to war. Apparently, Polk considered the rewards worth the risk. The territory at stake included not only Texas, but part of New Mexico and smaller portions of Oklahoma, Kansas, Colorado, and Utah.

The Texans themselves had requested statehood. As a self-governing republic, Texas was sandwiched between larger neighbors. The republic would be overshadowed and possibly threatened from North and South. According to James Polk, the situation would be equally uncomfortable for the United States. He explained in a campaign speech that an independent Texas would represent a "danger to [American] safety and future peace."[2]

Texas Statehood and Manifest Destiny

As it happened, Polk did not have to push Texas statehood through Congress. Outgoing President John

Tyler took care of that for him. Tyler knew that Texas ratification could never win the necessary two-thirds majority of the Senate. He therefore asked the House of Representatives to sponsor a joint resolution, which only required a simple majority of both houses. The resolution passed the House handily and squeaked through the Senate by two votes. President Tyler signed it on March 3, 1845, his last full day in office.

Abolitionists saw the admission of Texas as a power grab by the slave states. Former president John Quincy Adams called it "The heaviest [disaster] that ever befell myself and my country."[3] But journalist John L. O'Sullivan called it "manifest destiny." He coined the term in the July 1845 issue of *United States Magazine and Democratic Review*. He claimed that the enemies of the United States had tried to keep Texas out of the Union. They acted "in a spirit of hostile interference against us, for the [purpose] of thwarting our policy and hampering our power, limiting our greatness and checking the fulfillment of our manifest destiny to overspread the continent. . . ."[4]

Manifest destiny captured the American imagination. It allowed expansionists to justify everything from the murder and displacement of American Indians to wars of conquest. The United States was spreading the blessings of democracy across the continent, these expansionists claimed. They believed that the cause was just and God was on their side. The nation would thrust westward, the population would grow, and the economy would thrive.

A War of Conquest

On December 29, 1845, Texas became the twenty-eighth state in the Union. As many had expected, war with Mexico soon followed. On May 8, 1846, American and Mexican troops fought their first battle near the present-day city of Brownsville, Texas. Five days later, the United States made a formal declaration of war against Mexico.

Opponents of the war believed it was less about protecting Texas than grabbing territory from Mexico. Some people protested, scholars wrote essays, and politicians made speeches. Among those politicians was freshman congressman Abraham Lincoln of Illinois. His antiwar stand may well have cost him a second term in the House.

One of the most famous opponents of the war was writer and naturalist Henry David Thoreau. He went to jail for refusing to pay taxes that would be used to finance aggression against Mexico. In his famous essay "Civil Disobedience," Thoreau explained:

> when a sixth of the population of a nation [founded on] liberty are slaves, and a whole country is unjustly overrun and conquered by a foreign army . . . I think that it is not

Opponents of the Mexican War felt that American blood was being spilled only to gain more land for the slave state of Texas.

too soon for honest men to rebel and revolutionize. What makes this duty the more urgent is that fact that the country so overrun is not our own, but ours is the invading army.[5]

With these words, Thoreau made a powerful statement: that suffering a wrong was better than committing one. After going to jail for that belief, he declared that prison was "the true place for a just man" in an unjust society, and "the only house in a slave State in which a free man can abide with honor."[6]

President Polk and the Oregon Country

With the Mexican War underway, Polk turned his attention to Oregon. He wanted to settle this issue quickly. He needed an immediate success to shield his expansion program from criticism.

The Oregon country was perfect—acquiring it would extend the Northwest border to the Pacific Ocean. (It was an important part of Polk's plan: if the United States won the Mexican War, he intended to acquire California.) Best of all, from Polk's point of view, the United States already had a strong presence in Oregon. Since 1818, it had shared the territory with Britain. A treaty between the two nations provided for Oregon to "be free and open to vessels, citizens and subjects of both [nations]."[7]

Oregon was critical to President Polk's expansion plan. It would balance the admission of Texas as a slave state, thus reducing criticism from outraged Northerners. It would also get the manifest destiny program off to a good start. But as much as Polk valued Oregon, he did not want to risk war with Britain to get it. Fighting two enemies on two fronts would strain American resources to the breaking point.

The British were equally unwilling to fight. They did not want to risk their growing economic relationship with the United States. However, "fifty-four forty or fight" was nothing more than a clever campaign slogan to them. They would never agree to cede that much territory. The forty-ninth parallel was their limit.

Polk was not in a position to push for more. He knew that Congress would never agree to open a second front during the Mexican War. Caught between the dream of manifest destiny and the realities of politics, Polk accepted British terms.

On June 15, 1846, the United States and Britain signed a treaty setting the boundary at the forty-ninth parallel. This is the present border between the United States and Canada.

The Oregon Treaty drew a great deal of criticism. Southerners worried about Oregon the way Northerners worried about Texas. Neither side wanted to see the other gain an advantage in the ongoing dispute over slavery.

The Wilmot Proviso

On August 8, 1846, James I. McKay of North Carolina presented a $2 million appropriations bill to the House of Representatives. Its purpose was "to enable the President to conclude a treaty of peace with the Republic of Mexico."[8]

The request provoked an outburst of antiwar sentiment. Hugh White of New York called the war "unnecessary, uncalled for, and wholly unjustifiable."[9] He claimed its chief purpose was to acquire territory for the expansion of slavery. He challenged the slave-holding states to prove him wrong by banning slavery from all new territories. White may have been illustrating a point about the connection between expansionism and slavery.

At least one member of the House took the challenge seriously. David Wilmot, from Pennsylvania, proposed an amendment to the appropriations bill. It provided "That, as an expressed condition to the acquisition of any territory from the Republic of Mexico . . . neither slavery nor involuntary servitude shall ever exist in any part of said territory, except for crime, whereof the party shall first be duly convicted."[10]

The House of Representatives passed the bill with the Wilmot Proviso attached. The Senate failed to reach a vote before the session ended for the year. This split between the two houses was common in issues related to slavery.

The Northern states dominated in the House, where representation depended upon population. This gave antislavery advocates an edge. In the Senate, each state had two seats, regardless of its population.

The policy of admitting states in pairs—one slave, one free—practically guaranteed that the Senate would be deadlocked on issues related to slavery. President Polk was convinced that the Wilmot Proviso had doomed his appropriations bill.

He recorded the incident and his reaction to it in his diary:

> . . . after an exciting debate in the House a bill passed that body, but with a [harmful] and foolish amendment to the effect that no territory which might be acquired . . . from Mexico should ever be a slaveholding country. What connection slavery had with making peace with Mexico is difficult to [understand].[11]

The Lure of the West

Abolitionists did not find it difficult to understand the connection. They knew that President Polk wanted Mexican land, especially California. They also knew that the United States was winning the war. Polk would force Mexico to cede a huge block of its territory in return for peace.

After Mexico surrendered to the United States on February 2, 1848, the two governments signed the Treaty of Guadalupe Hidalgo. Under its terms, the United States acquired present-day California, Nevada, and Utah, along with parts of Arizona and New Mexico.

As the nation fulfilled its manifest destiny, spanning from the Atlantic to the Pacific, proslavery and antislavery factions continued to confront one another. They wanted the same thing: to spread their way of life through the new territories.

8

NORTH AND SOUTH: A CLASH OF CULTURES

When the nation had expanded from coast to coast, manifest destiny began to lose some of its luster. Instead of scrambling for more territory, American leaders began to focus on developing what they already had. As usual, the fate of slavery was an ongoing issue.

The year 1848 set the political stage for conflicts to come. The discovery of gold in California was followed quickly by the founding of a new political party. Both would have an impact on the abolitionist movement.

Slavery and the Golden State

On January 28, 1848, a Californian, John Marshall, trying to build a gristmill stumbled upon a deposit of gold. That find triggered the California gold rush.

People who lived nearby flocked to gold country as soon as they heard. Others came by wagon train or by boat. By 1849, thousands of gold seekers poured into California, and the legend of the forty-niners was born.

The forty-niners did not come as settlers, looking for land and the chance to build a new life. They came as fortune hunters. Most lived in small mining camps scattered through the foothills of the Sierra mountains. With no central government, the forty-niners made up rules as they went along, and broke those rules when it suited them. They created a wildly unpredictable economy. Everything was for sale, usually at unbelievably high prices. A prospector might pay as much as $1 for a single egg. That would be $19.99 in today's money.

Rowdy and uncivilized though it might be, gold rush California did have its good points. It offered a kind of freedom that had all but disappeared in the well-settled regions of the country. In this gold rush world, slavery simply did not belong. An article in *The Californian* of March 15, 1848, explained the reasons "why slavery should not be introduced here [in California]."[1] The first argument against slavery in California does not mince words: "it is wrong for [slavery] to exist anywhere."[2]

In September 1849, leading Californians met to create a constitution. The document would be delivered to Washington, D.C., along with California's request for statehood. The first section of the first article asserted that: "All men are by nature free and independent, and have certain inalienable rights, [including] enjoying and defending life and liberty, acquiring, possessing, and protecting property: and pursuing and obtaining safety and happiness."[3]

The list of rights that followed included a straightforward ban on slavery: "Neither slavery, nor involuntary servitude, unless for the punishment of crimes, shall ever be tolerated in this State."[4] This sentence echoed the Wilmot Proviso and the Northwest Ordinance of 1787. It also used the word "slavery," which the Founders of the United States so carefully avoided in the Constitution.

Horrified Southerners promptly organized to oppose California statehood. Just as quickly, Northerners gathered their forces to defend it. Feelings ran high on both sides of a looming constitutional crisis.

The Free Soil Party
On August 9, 1848, a group of concerned citizens met in Buffalo, New York, to form a new political party. They were mostly disillusioned Whigs and Democrats whose chief goal was to stop slavery from spreading into the newly acquired territories.

They chose the name "Free Soil Party," and crafted

one of the better mottoes in the history of American politics: "Free Soil, Free Speech, Free Labor, and Free Men."[5] They also nominated candidates for the upcoming elections, in which former president Martin Van Buren became their presidential nominee.

President Van Buren headed a group of reformist Democrats in New York. They became known as "Barnburners," after an old story about a farmer who burned down his barn to get rid of the rats. These Barnburners would disrupt political, social, or economic institutions in the name of reform. Going into the election of 1848, their chief target was the spread of slavery into new territories.

At the state Democratic convention in 1847, the Barnburners wanted to include the Wilmot Proviso in the party's platform. The convention was so divided on the issue that it could not reach a decision. On September 29, 1847, Van Buren and his fellow Barnburners walked out in protest.

As the Free Soil candidate, Van Buren received 291,616 votes, a respectable total for a third-party candidate. Many took this as a sign that attitudes toward slavery had begun to change.

The Last Compromise

Possibilities of change notwithstanding, California's desire to become a free state triggered what turned out to be the last compromise of the antebellum, or pre-Civil War, period. Both sides realized that California was special. Thanks to the gold rush, it had a growing population and a booming economy.

Most states became territories before they won statehood. However, the large territory of California had the resources to skip that intermediate stage. That alone was enough to frighten slave owners. California would come into the Union as a free state, and a powerful free state at that. On the other side of the controversy, abolitionists were determined to keep slavery out of the former Mexican territories.

The situation had all the makings of a full-scale political crisis. For Henry Clay, the Great Compromiser of the Missouri crisis, that was an irresistible challenge. Though in his seventies and largely retired from public life, Clay went to work. On January 29, 1850, he presented a complete package of legislation, called an omnibus bill, to the Senate.

From the moment debate began, strong words flew on both sides. For eight months, Congress debated. Sometimes, it seemed that the nation had turned a corner and compromise was no longer possible. Henry Clay's bill became hopelessly stalled.

The Senate never did pass Clay's "package." However, its main provisions eventually passed as five separate bills which:

Henry Clay was a powerful speaker and used this ability to push through the Compromise of 1850.

1) settled a boundary dispute involving Texas;

2) admitted California to the Union as a free state;

3) established the Utah and New Mexico territories. Where the issue of slavery would be decided by popular sovereignty when the states created from these territories could decide for themselves whether or not to have slavery;

4) passed a new fugitive slave law; and

5) banned the slave trade, but not slavery itself, in Washington, D.C.

These five bills made up the Compromise of 1850.

Though this compromise would keep the Union together for another ten years, it contained the seed of its own destruction.

The Fugitive Slave Act

The Fugitive Slave Act of 1850 required all citizens to aid in the identification and capture of runaway slaves. Those who defied this law faced substantial punishment. Federal marshals who refused to arrest suspected fugitives could be fined one thousand dollars. Civilians who helped or hid runaways faced the same fine, along with up to six months in jail.

Specially appointed commissioners decided the fate of accused runaways. There was no jury, nor could the captive testify in his or her own behalf. The person making the claim did not have to show documentary proof of ownership. Even the payment of commissioners worked against fairness. These officials were paid on a case-by-case basis. They earned ten dollars for ruling in favor of an owner, but only five for ruling in favor of a slave.

These faulty standards of proof endangered free blacks as well as slaves. Some slave catchers were not particular about who they grabbed. Any black person would do, regardless of his or her legal status.

Resistance and the Law

The Fugitive Slave Act gave Northerners a firsthand view of the brutalities of slavery. They saw the cruelty of the slave catchers, the grief of the fugitives, and the injustice of the system itself. Many Northerners who had never taken a position on slavery became committed abolitionists.

Others opposed the law simply because it turned free citizens into slavery's agents. These people generally felt that one compromise after another had helped the South and hurt the North. With the Fugitive Slave Act, many believed that the South had gone too far. For some Northern activists resisting the act became a point of honor.

Poet/philosopher Ralph Waldo Emerson called it a "filthy enactment [law]" and wondered how such legislation could be "made in the nineteenth century, by people who could read and write." He concluded with a resounding vow: "I will not obey it, by God!"[6] Emerson did not usually become involved in politics. The Fugitive Slave Act led him to join the abolitionists and call for resistance to the law. Emerson resisted by way of the podium and the pen.

Others found more direct ways of protest. Many took to the streets to demonstrate their opposition to glaring injustices. One of the most memorable of these demonstrations occurred in Boston on May 24, 1854.

The capture of runaway slave Anthony Burns triggered a noisy protest on the courthouse steps. Some two thousand people gathered there to support him and demand his release.

President Franklin Pierce responded by sending in the marines. These soldiers faced some fifty thousand outraged Bostonians, roaring their disapproval as authorities marched Anthony Burns to Boston Harbor. There, a ship waited to return the young man to his owner in Virginia.

Unlike most cases, the story of Anthony Burns had a happy ending. After a black church raised thirteen hundred dollars to buy his freedom, Burns returned to Boston less than a year after his dramatic departure.

Reaction to the Burns case put the South on notice: the law alone could not protect the institution of slavery. In the North and the West, public opinion was turning against it. In the minds of many people, slavery was both barbaric and hopelessly outdated.

The Cost of Protecting Slavery

As opposition to slavery grew, so did the cost of maintaining the system. Enforcing the Fugitive Slave Law was an expensive proposition for both sides. Southerners had to pay for the pursuit and recapture of runaways. Northerners had to bear the cost of enforcing a law that many of them hated.

Runaway slaves Robert Burns and Anthony Sims were led through the streets of Boston by a group of soldiers. They had been captured and were about to be put on a steamship bound for South Carolina.

The Anthony Burns case in Boston illustrates the point. The pursuit and recapture of Burns and legal expenses came to more than forty thousand dollars. At the time, a young male slave was valued at around twelve hundred dollars.[7]

The Burns case was an extreme example of how far Southerners would go to assert their ownership rights. Slaves were an asset, like land or houses or farming equipment. Owners could buy, sell, and trade this human property. They could even use slaves as security for loans.

SOURCE DOCUMENT

Look at my case, I was stolen and made a slave as soon as I was born. No man had any right to steal me. That manstealer who stole me trampled on my dearest rights. He committed an outrage on the law of God; therefore his manstealing gave him no right in me, and laid me under no obligation to be his slave. God made me a man — not a slave; . . .[8]

Fugitive slave Anthony Burns was captured under the Fugitive Slave Law of 1850 and returned to his owner. He was also kicked out of his Church in Virginia. Upon discovering this, Burns spoke out against slavery in a letter to the church.

On the great plantations of the cotton South, abolition meant disaster. The wealthiest owners had a great deal of money tied up in slaves. In a single stroke, they could lose their workforce and their fortunes.

Even Southerners who did not own many slaves believed that their economic fate was tied to the system. They joined with the major owners to support and protect the peculiar institution. Northern abolitionists also closed ranks. Hopes for preserving the Union and avoiding war began to fade as both sides realized they were running out of compromises.

CHAPTER 9

THE ROAD TO DISUNION

BY THE 1850S, CONFLICTS OVER SLAVERY focused on the vast grassland of the Midwest. For many years, Americans had ignored these prairies. Would-be pioneers, settlers, and fortune-hunters passed through on their way to somewhere more profitable.

Gradually, though, the Midwest attracted people who planned to stay. They were practical, hard-working folk who wanted land and freedom. By the 1850s, the region known as Nebraska was ready to become a territory.

Senator Stephen A. Douglas of Illinois took up the cause. He did this with an eye to economic benefits. Developers were already planning a transcontinental railroad. In the not-too-distant future, it would cross the heartland of America, connecting the Atlantic and Pacific coasts.

If the railroad went through Nebraska, Chicago would be its hub, the place where train lines converged. If it passed farther to the south, then St. Louis would be the logical choice.

Where the railroad went, prosperity would follow. It would bring business and industry in its wake. Douglas needed cooperation from Southern lawmakers in order for his Nebraska plan to work. That meant he had to compromise with the slave states.

The Kansas-Nebraska Act

Douglas presented his Nebraska bill to Congress on January 4, 1854. It drew immediate fire from the South. Nebraska was north of the 36°30' line. That meant it was closed to slavery under the Missouri Compromise of 1820. Southerners complained that a free Nebraska would upset the balance between slave and free states.

In response to these concerns, Douglas revised his bill. The new version divided the territory into two parts—Kansas and Nebraska—and allowed them to decide on slavery for themselves. By using popular sovereignty, Douglas put the Kansas-Nebraska bill into direct conflict with the Missouri Compromise.

With the stroke of a pen, Stephen Douglas ignited

a hot controversy. He added a new clause to the bill that declared the Missouri Compromise "inoperable and void" because it violated "the principle of non-intervention by Congress."[1]

Abolitionist and former slave Frederick Douglass called the bill "an open invitation to a fierce and bitter strife."[2] Senator Salmon P. Chase called it the "violation of a sacred pledge" and a "criminal betrayal of precious rights."[3]

The Kansas-Nebraksa Act was passed on May 30, 1854. The new law changed the face of American

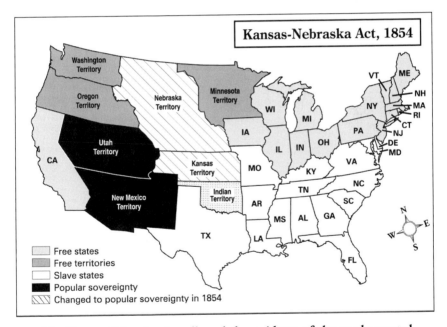

The Kansas-Nebraska Act allowed the residents of the newly created Kansas and Nebraska territories to decide for themselves whether or not to allow slavery within their borders.

politics. It contributed to the collapse of the Whig Party, the break between Northern and Southern Democrats, and the rise of the new Republican Party.

Bleeding Kansas

Frederick Douglass was right about the Kansas-Nebraska Act being an invitation to strife. The trouble began with the first territorial election. To ensure a proslavery legislature, hundreds of so-called "border ruffians" from Missouri poured into Kansas to stuff the ballot boxes.

Northerners raised thousands of dollars to send antislavery settlers into the Kansas territory. The territory soon divided into proslavery and antislavery factions. It was only a matter of time before violence between the two sides erupted.

On May 21, 1856, a proslavery mob went on a rampage in the antislavery town of Lawrence, Kansas. They burned the office of an antislavery newspaper and looted businesses. A few days later, a tall, fierce-eyed abolitionist named John Brown struck back. He and his men killed five proslavery settlers along the banks of Pottawatomie Creek.

After these first strikes, guerilla bands prowled Kansas, destroying life and property in the name of their cause. Newsman Horace Greeley called it "Bleeding Kansas" and the name fit all too well.[4]

Both sides of the conflict on Kansas were very passionate about their
views. This engraving depicts a confrontation at Fort Scott, Kansas.

In 1857, two rival groups held constitutional
conventions. Proslavery factions met in Lecompton,
while an antislavery group gathered in Topeka. The
Lecompton constitution supported the property rights
of slave owners, claiming that: "The right of property
is . . . higher than any constitutional [permission], and
the right of the owner of a slave to such slave and its
increase [offspring] is the same . . . as the right of the
owner of any property whatever."[5]

With the help of border ruffians, the proslavery
constitution won approval in Kansas. It did not fare as
well in Washington, D.C. The Senate approved it, but
the House of Representatives did not.

This rejection stalled Kansas statehood long enough for free-soil settlers to gain the upper hand in the Kansas legislature. In August 1858, Kansas voted down the Lecompton Constitution and again applied for admission to the Union, this time as a free state. On January 29, 1861, the request was granted.

The Dred Scott Decision

While the crisis in Kansas addressed large social issues, a smaller, more personal conflict developed around a slave named Dred Scott. His battle for freedom began in 1846, when Scott and his wife Harriet sued for their

SOURCE DOCUMENT

There is not the slightest danger of Kansas ever being a slave state These people are so much excited and so eager to avenge the wrongs for their friends who have been slaughtered in cold blood by the lawless devils They would fight till the last man would drop on the field but don't fear if the Missourians or the southern Statesmen attempt to rally again they wish they never had been such a country as Kansas.[6]

The author of this letter, I.T. Yunker is confident that the Free State supporters would win the battle for "Bleeding Kansas."

freedom. Their case soon came before the St. Louis Circuit Court.

It rested on the fact that the Scotts had lived in Wisconsin and Illinois for four years. Both were free states. The Scotts argued that living in this free society had made them free as well. The Circuit Court did not agree, and ruled against the Scotts. That first trial was just the beginning of a twelve-year saga.

The case went all the way to the Supreme Court. On March 7, 1857, the Justices issued a ruling that would shock the nation. Chief Justice Roger B. Taney wrote the opinion and read it in open court. Point by point, the Court demolished Dred Scott's case. It ruled that Congress did not have the power to ban slavery from any territory or state. The Missouri Compromise was, therefore, unconstitutional.

In a further ruling, the Justices held that African Americans, whether slave or free, were not entitled to the rights of citizens. Taney gave his opinion that African Americans had long been considered "beings of an inferior order" with "no rights which the white man was bound to respect." They could therefore be "bought and sold and treated as . . . ordinary article[s] of merchandise."[7]

This dredged up the old "persons or property" argument at its very worst. At a time when many people were coming to grips with the wrongs of slavery,

Although the Supreme Court did not grant Dred Scott his freedom, he was bought by a new owner shortly afterward and was freed two months later.

the Supreme Court gave them one more injustice to oppose.

"A House Divided Against Itself"

During the senatorial election of 1858 in Illinois, both the Dred Scott decision and the Kansas-Nebraska Act were fresh in the public mind. A little-known candidate for the Senate there regarded both as symptoms of a widening gulf between North and South.

In one of his most famous speeches, Abraham Lincoln warned voters in Springfield, Illinois, that the Union was in grave danger:

> A house divided against itself cannot stand. I believe this government cannot endure permanently half slave and half free. I do not expect the Union to be dissolved— I do not expect the house to fall—but I do expect it will cease to be divided. It will become all one thing, or all the other.[8]

Lincoln lost the election to the incumbent, or current officeholder, Stephen A. Douglas. However, he got his name, his image, and his ideas before the public in a series of debates with Douglas. By the end of the campaign, the self-educated lawyer from Springfield had positioned himself to make a run for the presidency in 1860.

By that time, both sides realized that the presidential election would also be a referendum on the Union. Southerners openly stated that if Lincoln were elected, the South would secede and form its own confederacy of states.

Slavery and the Economy in the Midwest Territories

Republicans were equally frank about their intentions. They condemned Southern claims that the Constitution allowed slavery to spread "into any or all of the territories of the United States."[9]

The Republicans asserted that "the normal condition of all the territory of the United States is that of freedom. . . . and we deny [any] authority . . . to give legal existence to slavery in any territory of the United States."[10]

Though Lincoln opposed slavery in principle, he did not want to abolish it in states where it was well established. He simply wanted to keep it from spreading. So long as the government did that, Lincoln believed that slavery would eventually disappear.

In the campaign of 1860, Lincoln did not stress moral arguments against the institution of slavery. Instead he pointed out the economic benefits of keeping the Midwest free. "We want [the territories] for the homes of free white people," he once said. "This they cannot be, to any considerable extent, if slavery shall be planted with them."[11] He stated that banning slavery would mean more jobs for free laborers.

Secession—A Parting of the Ways

As the election approached, Southerners prepared for the worst. They knew that their secession would mean war against a stronger and larger opponent.

The North had a growing economy and superior technology, along with well-developed banking, communication, and transportation networks. Its population was many times larger than that of the South. The Union had twenty-one states with a population of more than 20 million. The eleven states that seceded to form the Confederacy had a combined population of 9 million, including nearly 4 million slaves.[12]

In spite of this, Southerners did what they felt they had to do. On November 6, 1860, Abraham Lincoln was elected President of the United States. Six weeks later, on December 20, 1860, South Carolina became the first state to secede from the Union. It was soon followed by Mississippi, Florida, Alabama, Georgia,

Louisiana, and Texas, and later by Virginia, Arkansas, Tennessee, and North Carolina.

The Emancipation Proclamation

At the beginning of the war, Lincoln did not intend to deal with slavery. He focused entirely on saving the Union. As slaves fled their plantations by the thousands and fought alongside Union troops, Lincoln came to realize that there would be no place for slavery in this restored Union. The nation needed a fresh start, and that meant the complete abolition of slavery.

On January 1, 1863, Lincoln issued the famous Emancipation Proclamation, freeing "all persons held

This poster was used in Abraham Lincoln's 1860 bid for the presidency. His running mate, Hannibal Hamlin, is also pictured.

as slaves within any State . . . [that] shall then be in rebellion against the United States."[13] This presidential announcement did not immediately transform the lives of people living in slavery.

The proclamation did not free slaves in Maryland or Delaware—slave states that remained loyal to the Union. It could not be enforced in areas controlled by

Slaves in the South that were freed by invading Union forces were called contrabands. These contrabands take time to pose for a picture. Many contrabands worked to help the Union forces win the Civil War.

the Confederacy. Complete freedom of all slaves did not come until after the war when Congress passed the Thirteenth Amendment. It stated: "Neither slavery nor involuntary servitude, except as a punishment for crime whereof the party shall have been duly convicted, shall exist within the United States, or any place subject to their jurisdiction."[14]

With these simple but powerful words, Congress ended two hundred years of forced labor. The amendment achieved ratification on December 6, 1865. What began in seventeenth-century Jamestown doomed generations of African and African-American people to lives of bondage. Slavery itself grew from an informal system of bondage to a social institution. Along the way, it became the foundation of the Southern economy and way of life.

An amendment and the bloodiest war in American history finally destroyed the specter of slavery in a nation founded on principles of justice and equality.

1787	*July 13*: Northwest Ordinance passed.
1788	*June 21*: Constitution ratified by the states.
1790	*March 26*: Naturalization Act limits American citizenship to white immigrants.
1791	*December 12*: Bill of Rights ratified by the fourteen states at the time.
1793	*February 12*: President George Washington signs the Fugitive Slave Act.
1808	*January 1*: The slave trade is banned.
1820	*February 17*: Jesse B. Thomas proposes Missouri Compromise on slavery in the Louisiana Territory.
1820	*March 15*: Maine admitted to the Union as a free state.
1821	*August 10*: Missouri admitted to the Union as a slave state.
1845	*December 29*: Texas admitted to the Union as a slave state.
1846	*May 13*: United States formally declares war against Mexico. *June 15*: Britain cedes part of its Oregon territory to the United States. *August 8*: David Wilmot presents the Wilmot Proviso to the House Representatives.

1847	*September 29*: "Barnburners" protest the Democratic party's stand on slavery in the new territories.
1848	*February 2*: Mexico and the United States sign the Treaty of Guadalupe Hidalgo. *August 9*: The Free Soil Party is founded.
1849	*October 13*: California constitution bans slavery in the future state.
1850	*September 9 and 20*: Compromise of 1850 passed by Congress. California becomes a state.
1854	*January 4*: Stephen A. Douglas introduces a bill to create the Kansas and Nebraska territories.
1856	*May 21*: A proslavery mob loots the town of Lawrence, Kansas.
1857	*March 7*: Supreme Court renders the Dred Scott decision.
1860	*November 6*: Abraham Lincoln is elected president of the United States. *December 20*: South Carolina becomes the first state to secede from the Union.
1861	*January 29*: Kansas becomes the thirty-forth state admitted to the Union.
1863	*January 1*: President Lincoln issues the Emancipation Proclamation.
1864	*June 28*: Fugitive Slave Act repealed.
1865	*December 6*: Thirteenth amendment, freeing the slaves, ratified by the states.

CHAPTER NOTES

CHAPTER 1. THE BEGINNINGS OF AMERICAN SLAVERY

1. Hugh Thomas, *The Slave Trade: The Story of the Atlantic Slave Trade: 1440–1870* (New York: Simon & Schuster, 1997), p. 174.

2. "Constitution of the United States, Article IV, Sec. 2," *National Archives and Records Administration*, n.d., <http://www.archives.gov/national_archives_experience/constitution_transcript.html> (November 30, 2003).

3. "The Paris Peace Treaty (Peace Treaty of 1783)," *Archiving Early America*, n.d., <http://www.earlyamerica.com/earlyamerica/milestones/paris/text.html> (November 30, 2003).

4. "Declaration of Independence," *National Archives and Records Administration*, n.d., <http://www.archives.gov/national_archives_experience/declaration_transcript.html> (November 30, 2003).

5. Thomas, p. 21.

6. Ottobah Cugoano, *Narrative of the Enslavement of Ottobah Cugoano, a Native of Africa*, (Published by Himself, 1787), p. 124, Electronic Edition, "Documenting the American South," *The University of North Carolina at Chapel Hill Libraries*, 1999, <http://docsouth.unc.edu/neh/cugoano/cugoano.html> (March 5, 2004).

7. Peter Neilson, ed. *The Life and Adventures of Zamba, an African Negro King and His Experience of Slavery in South Carolina Written By Himself* (London: Smith, Elder & Co., 1847). Electronic ed., University of North Carolina at Chapel Hill, 2000. pp. 88-89. <http://docsouth.unc.edu/neh/neilson/neilson.html> (July 10, 2003).

8. *Africans in America Part 1: 1450–1750.* "The Terrible Transformation, Liverpool and the Slave Trade," n.d., <http://www.pbs.org/wgbh/aia/part1/1p318.html> (December 1, 2003).

CHAPTER 2. FROM SERVANTS TO SLAVES

1. "African Americans at Jamestown," *Colonial National Historical Park, United States Park Service,* n.d., <http://www.nps.gov/colo/Jthanout/AFRICANS.html> (December 1, 2003).

2. "Africans in America Part I: The Terrible Transformation, Virginia Recognizes Slavery," *Resource Bank,* n.d., <http://www.pbs.org/wgbh/aia/part1/1p262. html> (February 9, 2003).

3. "Africans in America Part I: Narratives, From Indentured Servitude to Racial Slavery," *Resource Bank,* n.d., <http://www.pbs.org/wgbh/aia/part1/1narr3.html> (February 9, 2003).

4. Ibid.

5. "From Indentured Servitude to Racial Slavery", *PBS Online: Africans in America,* © 1998, 1999, <http://www.pbs.org/wgbh/aia/part1/1narr3.html> (March 5, 2004).

6. Sojourner Truth, "Commencement of Isabella's Trials in Life," *The Narrative of Sojourner Truth* (1850) dictated by Sojourner Truth (ca. 1797-1883), ed. by Olive Gilbert <http://digital.library.upenn.edu/women/truth/1850/18509.html> (February 12, 2003).

7. Charles C. Jones. *The Religious Instruction of the Negroes in the United States* (Savannah: Thomas Purse, 1842), p. 159. Electronic ed., University of North Carolina at Chapel Hill Libraries. <http://docsouth.unc.edu/church/jones/jones.html> (July 10, 2003).

CHAPTER 3. SLAVERY AND THE FOUNDING FREEDOMS

1. "A Declaration of Rights," *Declaration of Independence.*

2. Don E. Fehrenbacher, *The Slaveholding Republic: An Account of the United States Government's Relations to Slavery* (New York: Oxford University Press, 2001), p. 16.

3. "The Articles of Association; October 20, 1774," *The American Constitution: A Documentary Record*, The Avalon Project at Yale Law School, <http://www.yale.edu/lawweb/avalon/contcong/10-20-74.htm> (February 25, 2003).

4. Ibid.

5. Ibid.

6. Ibid.

7. Thomas Jefferson, "Autobiography," *Thomas Jefferson: Writings* (New York: The Library of America, 1984), p. 22.

8. Ibid.

9. Ibid, p. 270.

10. "Thomas Jefferson: Legacy" Library of Congress, n.d., <http://www.loc.gov/exhibits/jefferson/jeffleg.html> (July 12, 2003).

11. Anonymous, "Response to Lord Dunmore's Proclamation: November 1775," *The American Revolution: Writings from the War of Independence* (New York: Library of America, 2001), p. 82.

12. John Laurens, Jr., "A Proposal to Free and Arm Slaves: January-February 1778," *The American Revolution: Writings from the War of Independence* (New York: Library of America, 2001), p. 410.

13. Alexander Hamilton, *Alexander Hamilton: Writings* (New York: Library of America, 2001), p. 56.

14. Ibid., pp. 56–57.

15. "George Washington, October 25, 1781, General Orders," *Library of Congress,* n.d., <http://memory.loc.gov/cgi-bin/query/r?ammem/mgw:@field(DOCID+@lit(gw230293))> (March 4, 2004).

16. Jefferson, p. 25.

CHAPTER 4. COMPROMISE AND THE CONSTITUTION

1. "James Madison: The Federal Convention of 1787," *The Annals of America, Volume 3: 1784-1796 Organizing a New Nation* (Chicago: Encyclopaedia Britannica, Inc., 1976), p. 100.

2. "The Debates in the Federal Convention of 1787 reported by James Madison: May 29," *The Avalon Project at Yale Law School,* n.d., <http://www.yale.edu/lawweb/avalon/debates/529.htm> (April 5, 2003).

3. *HIS 121 Research Document:* "Census Table 1. Slave Population in 1790," n.d., <http://www.vw.vccs.edu/vwhansd/HIS121Census1790.html> (April 9, 2003).

4. *Debate on the Constitution: Part One* (New York: Library of America, 1993), p. 968.

5. James Madison, "The Federalist No. 54," in *James Madison: Writings* (New York: Library of America, 1999), pp. 310–311.

6. James Madison, "Speech in the Virginia Ratifying Convention on the Slave Trade Clause," in *James Madison: Writings* (New York: Library of America, 1999), p. 391.

7. Ibid.

CHAPTER 5. SLAVERY IN A GROWING NATION

1. "The Northwest Ordinance," *The Annals of America, Volume 3: 1784–1796 Organizing a New Nation* (Chicago: Encyclopaedia Britannica, Inc., 1976), p. 195.

2. Ibid, p. 196.

3. Ibid, p. 194.

4. Eric Foner, *The Story of American Freedom* (New York: W.W. Norton & Company, 1998), p. 36.

5. "The Constitution" in *James Madison: Writings* (New York: Library of America, 1999), p. 882.

6. Ibid.

7. Don E. Fehrenbacher, *The Slaveholding Republic: An Account of the United States Government's Relations to Slavery* (New York: Oxford University Press, 2001), p. 142.

8. Ibid, pp. 141–142.

9. Absalom Jones, "Jones's sermon on the abolition of the international slave trade," *PBS Online: Africans in America,* © 1998, 1999, <http://www.pbs.org/wgbh/aia/part3/3h92t.html> (March 5, 2004).

CHAPTER 6. MISSOURI AND THE WESTWARD EXPANSION

1. "Tallmadge's Speech to Congress," *Annals of Congress, the Fifteenth Congress Second Session, V. 1* (Washington, D.C.: Government Printing Office, 1855), pp. 1203–1205. <http://www.wadsworth.com/history_d/special_features/ext/ap/chapter9/9.3.tallmadge.html> (January 30, 2004).

2. Charles Pinckney, "Speech to Congress, 1820," *Annals of Congress, the Sixteenth Congress First Session, V. 2* (Washington, D.C.: Governmental Printing Office, 1855), p. 1325. <http://www.wadsworth.com/history_d/template/student_resources/0030724791_ayers/sources/ch09/9.3.pickney.html> (March 5, 2004).

3. Ibid., p. 1327.

4. Ibid., p. 1328.

5. Thomas Jefferson, "A Firebell in the Night," *The Annals of America, Volume 4: 1797–1820 Domestic Expansion and Foreign Entanglements* (Chicago: Encyclopaedia Britannica, Inc., 1976), p. 603.

6. Ibid.

7. Howard Dodson, "How Slavery Helped Build a World Economy," *National Geographic News*, February 3, 2003, <http://news.nationalgeographic.com/news/2003/01/0131_030203_jubilee2.html> (December 6, 2003).

8. Joseph Jones, *Agricultural Resources of Georgia. Address Before the Cotton Planters Convention of Georgia at Macon, December 13, 1860,* (Augusta, Ga.: Steam Press of Chronicle and Sentinel, 1861), p. 5, Electronic Edition, "Documenting the American South," *The University of North Carolina at Chapel Hill Libraries*, 2001, <http://docsouth.unc.edu/imls/agriculture/agriculture.html> (March 5, 2004).

CHAPTER 7. SLAVERY AND MANIFEST DESTINY

1. "James K. Polk: The Annexation of Texas and Oregon," *The Annals of America Vol. 7: Manifest Destiny* (Chicago: Encyclopaedia Britannica, 1976), p. 286.

2. Ibid., p. 287.

3. Don E. Fehrenbacher, *The Slaveholding Republic: An Account of the United States Government's Relations to Slavery* (New York: Oxford University Press, 2001), p. 125.

4. John L. O'Sullivan, "Our Manifest Destiny," *The Annals of America: Vol. 7 1841–1849: Manifest Destiny* (Chicago: Encyclopaedia Britannica, 1976), p. 289.

5. Henry David Thoreau, "Civil Disobedience," *The Web of American Transcendentalism* (Virginia Commonwealth University, 2002) <http://www.vcu.edu/engweb/transcendentalism/index.html> (September 5, 2003).

6. Ibid.

7. James Clotier, "On This Day in Oregon," n.d., <http://www.onthisdayinoregon.com/10_20.html> (September 6, 2003).

8. Michael A. Morrison, *Slavery and the American West: The Eclipse of Manifest Destiny and the Coming of the Civil War* (Chapel Hill, NC: University of North Carolina Press, 1997), p. 40.

9. Ibid., p. 41.

10. "David Wilmot Helped End Slavery in America," *Bradford County Historical Society,* n.d., <http://www.wyalusing.net/poi/davidwilmot.html> (February 20, 2004).

11. James Knox Polk, *The Diary of a President 1845–1849, Covering the Mexican War, the Acquisition of Oregon, and the Conquest of California and the Southwest,* ed. Allan Nevins, (London: Longmans, Green, 1952), p. 138.

CHAPTER 8. NORTH AND SOUTH: A CLASH OF CULTURES

1. Rockwell D. Hunt, Ph.D., "How California Came To Be Admitted," *San Francisco Chronicle*, September 9, 1900 <http://www.sfmuseum.org/hist5/caladmit.html> (September 14, 2003).

2. Ibid.

3. "California constitution of 1849," n.d., <http://www.ss.ca.gov/archives/level3_const1849txt.html> (September 12, 2003).

4. Ibid.

5. Mark Lause, "The Free Soil Party," *Lause's Links*, n.d., <http://www.geocities.com/CollegePark/Quad/6460/dir/848frso.html> (September 16, 2003).

6. "Ralph Waldo Emerson: On the Fugitive Slave Law," Introduction, *The Annals of America Volume 8, 1850–1857: A House Dividing* (Chicago: Encyclopaedia Britannica, 1976), p. 261.

7. "Brookline in the Civil War," from John Gould Curtis, *History of the Town of Brookline* (Boston: Houghton Mifflin Company, 1933) <http://www.garrenshay.com/ur/history.htm> (December 10, 2003).

8. Anthony Burns, "Letter from Anthony Burns to the Baptist Church," *PBS Online: Africans in America*, © 1998, 1999, <http://www.pbs.org/wgbh/aia/part4/4h2917t.html> (March 5, 2004).

CHAPTER 9. THE ROAD TO DISUNION

1. "An Act to Organize the Territories of Nebraska and Kansas," *Avalon Project at Yale Law School*, n.d., <http://www.yale.edu/lawweb/avalon/kanneb.htm> (December 23, 2003).

2. Quoted in "Stephen Douglas," *Spartacus Educational*, n.d. <http://www.spartacus.schoolnet.co.uk/USAdouglas.htm> (September 25, 2003).

3. Salmon P. Chase, "Opposition to the Kansas-Nebraska Bill," *The Annals of America Volume 8 1850–1857: A House Dividing* (Chicago: Encyclopaedia Britannica, 1976), p. 251.

4. "Bleeding Kansas," *U.S. History.com*, n.d., <http://www.u-s-history.com/pages/h84.html> (September 12, 2003).

5. Frank W. Blackmar, ed., "Constitutions," *Kansas: a cyclopedia of state history, embracing events, institutions, industries, counties, cities, towns, prominent persons, etc. ... /*, Vol. 1, n.d., <http://skyways.lib.ks.us/genweb/archives/1912/c/constitutions.html> (September 24, 2003).

6. I.T. Yunker, "War Letters, 'Bleeding Kansas': I.T. Yunker," *Kansas State Historical Society*, © 2001, <http://www.kshs.org/ms/warletters/yunker.htm> (March 5, 2004).

7. Roger Taney, "The Dred Scott Decision," *Digital History* (University of Houston, 2003) <http://www.digitalhistory.uh.edu/documents/documents_p2.cfm?doc=23> (September 27, 2003).

8. Abraham Lincoln, "House Divided" Speech. June 16, 1858. *The History Place.* <http://www.historyplace.com/lincoln/divided.htm> (September 28, 2003).

9. "Party Platforms of 1860," *Annnals of America Volume 9 1858–1865: The Crisis of the Union* (Chicago: Encyclopaedia Britannica, 1976), p. 189.

10. Ibid., pp. 189–190.

11. Thomas J. DiLorenzo, "Rewriting Economic History," n.d., <http://www.lewrockwell.com/dilorenzo/dilorenzo17.html> (December 10, 2003).

12. "A Nation Divided," *The History Place, The U.S. Civil War 1861–1865*, n.d., <http://www.historyplace.com/civilwar/> (September 28, 2003).

13. Abraham Lincoln, "The Emancipation Proclamation: By the President of the United States of America," n.d., <http://www.nps.gov/malu/documents/lincoln_emancipation_proclamation.html> (September 28, 2003).

14. "Constitution of the United States: Amendment XIII," Thomas Legislative Information on the Internet, n.d., <http://memory.loc.gov/const/amend.html> (December 11, 2003).

✧ Glossary ✧

AMENDMENT—A formal change or addition to an existing law or constitution.

ANTEBELLUM—The period before the American Civil War.

ARISTOCRAT—A member of the highest social group.

BICAMERAL—A legislature with two chambers or "houses."

BOYCOTT—Refusing to deal with a particular person or group.

CONCEDE—To yield a point, or acknowledge as true.

CUSTOMS—A tax on imported goods.

DISUNION—Separation, usually with discord.

EMANCIPATE—To set free.

FUGITIVE—One who runs away or flees, usually from the law.

HERESY—Opinions or doctrines that conflict with established belief.

HOUSEHOLD ECONOMY—An economy based upon self-sufficient family units.

INALIENABLE—Cannot be taken away or transferred to another.

INDENTURED SERVITUDE—The state of being bound to service for a specified period of time.

ISOLATE—To set apart from others.

LATITUDE—In geography, imaginary lines circling the earth; measured in degrees north or south of the equator.

SECEDE—To leave an organization or nation.

FURTHER READING

Burchard, Peter. *Lincoln and Slavery*. New York: Atheneum Books for Young Readers, 1999.

Center for Civic Education, ed. *We the People . . . the Citizen and the Constitution*. Calabasas, Calif.: Center for Civic Education, 2000.

Collier, Christopher and James Lincoln Collier. *The Cotton South and the Mexican War, 1835–1850*. New York: Benchmark Books, 1998.

——*Slavery and the Coming of the Civil War, 1831–1861*. New York: Benchmark Books, 2000.

Freedman, Russel. *In Defense of Liberty: The Story of America's Bill of Rights*. New York: Holiday House, 2003.

Gunderson, Cory. *The Dred Scott Decision*. Edina, Minn.: Abdo Publishers, 2004.

Meltzer, Milton. *The Cotton Gin*. New York: Benchmark Books, 2003.

Olson, Kay Melchisedech. *Africans in America, 1619–1865*. Mankato, Minn.: Bridgestone Books, 2002.

Torr, James D., ed. *Slavery: Opposing Viewpoints in World History*. San Diego, Calif.: Greenhaven Press, 2004.

Zeinert, Karen. *Tragic Prelude: Bleeding Kansas*. North Haven, Conn.: Shoe String Press, 2001.

❖ INTERNET ❖
ADDRESSES
❦

"AFRICAN-AMERICAN PAMPHLET COLLECTION,"
THE LIBRARY OF CONGRESS, October 31, 2003,
<http://memory.loc.gov/ammem/aapchtml/
aapchome.html> (June 3, 2004)

"AFRICANS IN AMERICA/PART 4/RESOURCE BANK
CONTENTS," PBS ONLINE, n.d., <http://www.
pbs.org/wgbh/aia/part4/index.html> (June 3, 2004).

"SLAVES AND THE COURTS, 1740-1860," THE
LIBRARY OF CONGRESS, April 5, 2002, <http://
memory.loc.gov/ammem/sthtml/sthome.html>

❖ HISTORIC ❖
SITES

FORT SCOTT NATIONAL HISTORIC SITE
P.O. Box 918
Fort Scott, KS 66701-0918
(620) 223-0310
E-mail: fosc_superintendent@nps.gov
<http://www.nps.gov/fosc/info.htm>

OLD COURTHOUSE (where the trial of Dred Scott began)
c/o Jefferson Expansion Memorial
11 N. 4th St.
St. Louis, MO 63102
(314) 655-1700
<http://www.nps.gov/jeff/about.html>

U.S. CAPITOL BUILDING
Washington, DC
(202) 225-6827
<http://www.aoc.gov/visit/visit_overview.htm>

I N D E X